Praise For The Wholeness of a Life Redeemed

The Wholeness of a Life Redeemed is a tender, courageous memoir that holds space for the complexities of trauma, healing, and self-returning. Shanna writes with a softness that makes even the most difficult moments feel seen and understood, inviting the reader to witness not just what she survived but how she slowly rebuilt her sense of safety, identity, and worth. Her vulnerability offers comfort, validation, and possibility to anyone who has ever felt broken or disconnected from themselves. This is a deeply compassionate book that reminds us that healing is gradual, personal, and always within reach.
—Kayley Hamilton, 2x Emmy Award–Winning Journalist & Founder of *UPLVL PR Agency*

***

Reading this book was deeply moving for me. It's raw, honest, and unfiltered in a way that feels incredibly brave. It doesn't rush healing or try to make pain sound pretty, instead it honors the full weight of what it means to survive trauma and slowly rebuild a life from the inside out. There were moments that felt heavy, but also moments that felt sacred, because the truth is that healing often happens in the quiet, uncomfortable spaces we'd rather avoid.

What stood out to me most is how clearly God's hand is present throughout this story.. not in perfection, but in perseverance. You see Him in the moments where the author keeps going when it would've been easier to give up, in the courage to set boundaries, in the decision to choose sobriety, stillness, and truth over numbing and escape. This book is a beautiful reminder that God doesn't wait for us to be whole before He meets us - He meets us right in the middle of the mess and walks with us through the rebuilding.

This story is powerful not because it avoids darkness, but because it shows how redemption can grow even there. It offers hope to anyone who has ever felt broken, unworthy, or too far gone, and gently reminds the reader that restoration is possible. This is not just a story of survival, it's a testimony of God's faithfulness and the strength that can be found when we finally choose ourselves and allow Him to do the healing work.

—**Meredith Hutson,** Transformation Coach,
Getfitwithmer

***

This book is a raw and reverent testimony of what happens when God meets a woman in the ruins and refuses to leave her there. *The Wholeness of a Life Redeemed* does not offer polished answers or shallow encouragement. It offers truth. Through courage, honesty, and surrender, Shanna Daley invites the reader into a sacred process where brokenness is acknowledged, responsibility is faced, and redemption is received rather than earned. This story reflects the heart of the Gospel: that God does not waste pain, that healing is possible without denial, and that wholeness is not found through striving but through being restored by His love. For anyone who has ever wondered if their story could still be redeemed, these pages stand as quiet, steady proof that God is faithful to make all things new.

—Pastor Angela Agia

The Wholeness of a Life Redeemed

Shanna Daley

Published by KHARIS PUBLISHING,
an imprint of KHARIS MEDIA LLC.

ISBN-13: 978-1-63746-696-4

ISBN-10: 1-63746-696-X

Library of Congress Control Number: 2026935282

All KHARIS PUBLISHING products are available at special quantity discounts for bulk purchases for sales promotions, premiums, fund-raising, and educational needs. For details, contact:

Kharis Media LLC
Tel: +1 (331) 312-2376
support@kharispublishing.com
www.kharispublishing.com

To the woman at the well, whose story reminds us that no past is too heavy, no shame too deep, and no heart too weary to be met by Jesus. Like her, we have all found ourselves standing at the well, carrying our brokenness, our regrets, and our thirst for something greater. May this book be a reminder that He sees us, knows us fully, and offers the living water that restores, redeems, and makes us whole.

Trigger Warning!

A vivid description of sexual assault is forthcoming in Chapter 4, and sensitive readers should consider skipping it or read it with care.

Foreword

Shanna Daley's personal story of brokenness and redemption offers a raw, honest, unvarnished look at the harsh consequences of a life lived by the wrong compass. It is not a story that ends in despair. It is a testimony of hope for those who feel trapped or disqualified by the past.

In these pages, Shanna shares a journey of redemption and transformation that reminds us God does not discard what is broken. Instead, He reshapes it. Her story points to a truth scripture has long made clear, healing and renewal are possible when we are willing to place ourselves in God's hands.

This is a journey within reach of anyone willing to climb onto the potter's wheel and remain there while God remakes the old and broken into something new and beautiful. As you read, you will be invited not only to witness that work, but to consider what it might look like in your own life.

—**Larry Osborne,** Author and Pastor, *North Coast Church*

Contents

Introduction

Before the Bloom

There was a time when I didn't think I would make it. Not just through the day, but through life itself.

I carried a weight so heavy it crushed the breath out of me, and there were nights when I laid in bed wondering if my absence would be easier for everyone else than my presence. I knew how to smile, perform, and pretend, but behind closed doors, I was breaking. The worst part was, I believed that broken was all I would ever be.

If you've ever stood in that place-where the mirror reflects not who you are, but who you fear you'll always be-you know the ache I'm talking about. The kind of ache that seeps into your bones, convinces you freedom is for other people and that joy is something you weren't built for. For so long, I thought my story was already written, and because of what I was born into, the trauma I carried, the mistakes I made, the wounds I endured, there was no room left for redemption. I thought my future would always taste like my past.

Here is the truth I now know, the truth this book dares to tell. You are not forever bound to the pain you were handed. I am not forever defined by the choices I made in fear, desperation, and survival. We are not sentenced to repeat the same cycles just because they're familiar. There is another way. I am living proof of it.

My story is not one of perfection. It is one of fire, ashes, rebuilding, and the slow, quiet miracle of becoming. This is not a tale of someone who figured it all out and lived a flawless life. It is the testimony of someone who nearly gave up but chose, against all odds, to plant something new - to take the ruins of what was and believe that God could grow beauty there.

This book is not about the version of me that smiled on the outside. It is about the me that trembled in the dark, that fought panic starting at eight years old, that questioned whether she belonged in her own family, that searched for love in all the wrong places because she didn't yet believe she was worthy of it. It is about the woman who walked through betrayal, abuse, loss, and loneliness, and still learned how to rise.

However, it is also about something bigger. It is about the God who took my brokenness and breathed life into it. It is about the land, animals, ordinary mornings, and quiet evenings that whispered to me that joy is not earned, but is received. It is about how the smallest acts of courage-choosing honesty, boundaries, and forgiveness-become the roots of a whole new life.

You will not find glamor here. You will not find easy answers or a neatly wrapped bow tied around the pain. What you will find is truth: raw, unfiltered, and at times, uncomfortable. You will find the weight of survival and the tenderness of healing. You will find the mess of becoming and the miracle of redemption. And if you read closely enough, you may find yourself, too.

Because my story is not just mine. It belongs to anyone who has ever wondered if they were too broken to be whole. To anyone who has questioned if joy could exist after devastation. To anyone who has carried the lie that they were unworthy of love, of peace, of freedom. If you are holding this book in your hands, perhaps you are carrying that question even now.

Here is my invitation to you. Keep reading. Let these words remind you that you are not alone. Let my journey show you that even when the soil looks barren, seeds are already taking root beneath the surface. Let this testimony be a light for your own path, a whisper to your own weary heart that there is more for you, too.

This is not just a story of survival. It is a story of redemption, wholeness, and finding joy in unexpected places and peace in the middle of storms. It is a story of planting new roots and watching them grow into something strong enough to weather every season.

This is my story. But it might just change how you see yours.

Chapter 1

The Beginning

I grew up in California during the 1980s. I was raised in a middle class family, cared for, and surrounded by the comforts that most families take for granted. On the surface, it looked normal, happy even. Beneath that surface, I carried a quiet anxiety that no one could see.

My parents were very young when they had me. In many ways, they were still growing up themselves. They were figuring out how to make ends meet, how to communicate, and how to carry the weight of responsibility they hadn't been fully prepared for. They loved me. I never doubted that. However, love doesn't erase the strain of immaturity or inexperience. Their relationship often carried the sharp edges of two people trying to navigate adulthood without the tools to do so. Tension could creep into the walls of our home, sometimes in loud, obvious ways and sometimes in silence that pressed down heavier than words. I can remember nights when voices rose behind closed doors, the sound muffled but sharp enough to set my heart racing. Children don't need words to understand conflict. The air changes, the walls seem thinner, and suddenly even a bedroom door closing loudly can feel like a warning.

I understand now that they were human, like all of us, with their own sets of struggles, traumas, and experiences that shaped the way they approached parenthood. They did the best they could with what they had, but their own baggage often cast shadows over my childhood. Their expectations of what family life should be, how children should behave, and what it meant to be "good enough" sometimes felt overwhelming. It wasn't a lack of love. They loved me, but their projections and standards made it hard for me to feel like I fully measured up.

Recognizing my parents as people, with flaws and histories of their own, has been a crucial part of understanding myself and forgiving the past. I remember one evening when my father lost his temper over something minor, slamming a kitchen drawer in frustration. My mother rushed to calm him, and I huddled in my bedroom, feeling both frightened and powerless. In those quiet moments afterward, I would reflect on their struggles, realizing that they were shaped by their own experiences, often hidden beneath smiles and routine. These early lessons in empathy, though mixed with fear, would later guide me in understanding human complexity and forgiving myself for my own mistakes.

Even with that understanding, I never really felt like I fit neatly inside my family. From a very young age, I carried the weight of trying to make them proud, as if my worth hinged on invisible checklists I couldn't see but knew I was failing to complete. I wanted their love so badly. Though I know they loved me, at the time it felt like something was always just out of reach. The harder I tried, the more it seemed to slip through my fingers. The pain of feeling like I wasn't enough became something I carried into the rest of my life.

My little sister's arrival only deepened that ache. She looked like my mother's reflection, red-haired and freckled, the living embodiment of beauty that others couldn't help but notice. Next to her, I felt misplaced, like a puzzle piece jammed into the wrong picture. Her striking resemblance to my mom drew attention everywhere we went, and in contrast, I felt overlooked, different, out of place, and often very isolated.

That difference became the soil where insecurity grew. Sometimes, in jokes meant to be funny, people would say things like I looked like "the milkman's baby." It was casual and innocent to them, but to a child, those words bury themselves deep. They linger, shaping the way you see yourself and your worth. I remember looking in the bathroom mirror after one of those comments, tracing the shape of my nose or the curve of my cheek, wondering if there was something fundamentally wrong with the way I looked. I wondered if there was something about me that would make others love me less, something I couldn't change no matter how hard I tried.

Even as a child, I remember noticing the small things that felt off balance. The way shadows fell in our house in the late afternoon, how the creak of the floorboards at night made me pause, listening for sounds that weren't there. The hum of the refrigerator, the distant barking of a neighbor's dog, the smell of my mother's perfume lingering in the hallway. All of it became part of a sensory world that heightened my awareness and made me hyper-conscious of everything around me. It was as if my mind had learned early to scan for threats or imperfections, even when there were none. My childhood wasn't just a time of learning and playing. It became training in vigilance and reading the atmosphere of a room before I dared to relax.

By the time I was eight, I was lying awake at night, staring at the ceiling, my small mind spinning with thoughts that didn't belong to childhood. I thought about life, what it meant to exist, to come into this world, and eventually to leave it. Those questions should have been years away, but they pressed on me early, heavy and suffocating. Sleep came in fragments, if at all. I tried to distract myself by counting the ceiling tiles, repeating cartoon lines I'd memorized, or whispering little stories into the darkness. The "what ifs" would inevitably creep back. *What if life meant nothing? What if death was forever? What if love could disappear?* My heart would pound beneath the blankets, and I'd stare into the dark, desperate for quiet, wishing someone could silence the thoughts I couldn't escape.

As I moved from childhood into my teenage years, the feelings of not fitting in didn't go away. They intensified. My body developed much earlier than most of my friends. By the time I was twelve, I had curves and a double-D chest, features that set me apart in ways I wasn't always prepared to handle. The attention I started to receive from men made me feel, for the first time, a kind of validation. It was intoxicating to be seen, to be noticed. It was also confusing and, at times, frightening.

I began to link my worth to the way my body could attract others. Without fully understanding it, I allowed myself to believe that sexual attention was what made me valuable as a person. That belief planted a quiet but powerful idea that my worth was defined not by who I was, but how others saw me. I remember feeling a mix of pride and fear when boys whispered compliments. I felt both powerful and exposed in the same breath. That tension settled into my heart, shaping many of my decisions and relationships later in life.

This mindset carried me down a path that would become difficult to navigate. By high school, the attention and validation I had grown accustomed to evolved into struggles with sex, boundaries, and control. It eventually led to pregnancy at a young age and the heartache, shame, and confusion that came with it. These experiences didn't just shape my teenage years. They left a lasting imprint on how I would relate to relationships, intimacy, and even myself for years to come.

School was its own battlefield. On the surface, I looked like a typical teenager, moving through classes and friendships, laughing in the hallways, and keeping up appearances. Internally, I was constantly measuring myself against everyone around me. Friends, classmates, and even the adults who should have been guiding me became silent judges in my mind. Every interaction was a test. *Was I pretty enough? Was I smart enough? Was I funny enough? Did I belong?*

The attention I received from boys complicated things further. Some of it felt flattering, even exhilarating, but it also stirred a dangerous mix of pride and anxiety. I wanted to be seen, to feel desirable, but I didn't yet understand that attention alone couldn't define my worth. It was a fragile validation that could vanish in an instant, leaving behind shame, self-doubt, and the lingering question: *Am I enough if no one is looking?*

Friendships were equally tricky. I wanted connection and acceptance, but insecurity often sabotaged me. I would compare myself constantly to my friends, my sister, and girls I didn't even know. That comparison created a quiet but persistent pressure to perform, to present myself in a way that others would approve of. It was exhausting and isolating, a constant balancing act between craving love and fearing rejection. I remember one sleepover when I sat in the corner while other girls giggled and whispered. I wanted to join, to belong, but my voice seemed to stick in my throat. The laughter around me only amplified the silence inside me.

Then I met him, my son's father. For the first time in my life, someone made me feel truly seen. Not the version of me that was defined by my body, my insecurities, or the ways I sought validation from the outside world. He saw me, the real me, the parts of me I had hidden even from myself. It was the first time I experienced love that felt unconditional, genuine, and unwavering.

I didn't know at the time how to fully comprehend what it meant to be loved in that way. I had never experienced it before. Most of my life had been about striving, performing, or seeking approval. But here was someone who simply wanted to love me, not the image I projected, but the person underneath it all. His love felt like both a refuge and a mirror, showing me not only who I was but also who I could become.

Chapter 2

Love Before I Knew How

My pregnancy with my son came during my senior year of high school. It was unplanned, which brought fear, uncertainty, and a profound sense of responsibility. Amidst all that, it was also incredibly beautiful. That life growing inside me was born from something pure. It came from a connection between two flawed people, each carrying their own brokenness, yet able to create something meaningful together.

Even knowing I was unprepared, even knowing that I would struggle to handle the depth of the love being offered to me, I was changed. The experience challenged, terrified, and humbled me, but it also revealed what love could look like when it is not conditional or transactional. It showed me that even in brokenness, there is space for beauty, for connection, and for hope.

Being a teen mom was far harder than I could have imagined. Not just because of my age, but because of the mental and emotional storm that accompanied it. The joy of holding my son for the first time, knowing I had created something so beautiful and real, was constantly shadowed by fear, anxiety, and a deep sense of inadequacy. I loved him fiercely, but I also felt unprepared, fragile, and terrified that I would fail him. I remember sitting in the hospital room, staring at his tiny face, and feeling both awe and panic. How could someone like me be trusted with something so perfect?

Postpartum depression hit me with a force I had never experienced before. Some days I could barely get out of bed. Other days I moved through life on autopilot, smiling and pretending everything was fine. Inside, my mind was a battlefield, invaded by ideas I never imagined confronting, including the persistent pull toward ending my own life, while the anxiety I had carried since childhood intensified. The weight of responsibility, layered with insecurities that had haunted me for years, felt almost unbearable.

Every milestone of his first year-his first smile, first steps, first words-was both a blessing and a reminder of how vulnerable I felt. I would ask myself, *Am I enough? Can I really do this?* For the first time, I realized that love alone was not always enough to save you from yourself. I needed support, guidance, and courage that I did not always know how to summon. The joy of his laugh was like sunlight, but the shadows inside me often threatened to swallow it.

As life moved forward, my son's father and I eventually got married. At the time, it felt like a continuation of the love and hope that had first drawn us together. It felt like a promise that our family could thrive despite the challenges we had already faced. I quickly learned that marriage was far more complicated than the idea I had imagined.

I was young, insecure, and still carrying the weight of my past. My anxiety, need for validation, and lingering fear of not being enough came with me into that marriage. I did not fully understand what unconditional love really meant-not just receiving it, but giving it in a way that could sustain a partnership. My insecurities often drove me to seek attention in ways that he, no matter how much he loved me, could not provide. In that mismatch, cracks began to form.

It became clear, painfully so, that I was not yet equipped to navigate the challenges of marriage. My immaturity, inability to manage my expectations, and constant struggle with self-worth made it impossible for the relationship to flourish the way it could have. I made many mistakes that contributed to the dissolution of our marriage. Eventually, we separated, and I became a single mom. Losing that partnership was heartbreaking, but it was also a turning point. It forced me to confront myself in a way I had not before. I had to look at my insecurities, my patterns, and my inability to fully receive and give love, and take responsibility for my own growth.

Being a single mom brought its own set of challenges and lessons. I was navigating life, work, and parenthood alone, often feeling stretched thin and questioning whether I could manage it all. At the same time, it was empowering. I began to recognize my own strength, ability to persevere, and capacity to love unconditionally. I was no longer loving because someone else validated me. I was loving because I had to, for my son and eventually for myself. I learned how to hold my head up even when exhaustion pulled me down, and how to celebrate small victories like paying bills on time or getting through a long day without breaking down.

What I was learning then was not how to be whole, but how to survive. I learned how to keep going even when I felt empty, how to push through fear without knowing what waited on the other side, and how to carry responsibility that felt far heavier than my years. I learned how to function through exhaustion, how to quiet my own needs to meet someone else's, and how to keep moving forward even when I doubted myself at every turn.

Looking back, the marriage and its end were not failures. They were crucial lessons in understanding myself, my needs, and the importance of self-awareness and emotional maturity. They were a bridge between the struggles of my youth and the person I was destined to become. They pushed me to grow into a mother, a woman, and eventually, someone who could rise from hardship into strength and clarity.

Looking back now, I can say that being a single mom was both humbling and empowering, a season that taught me how strong I could be when circumstances left me no choice. But even though I had begun to glimpse my strength, the truth is, I wasn't there yet. Not fully. On the outside, I looked like a young woman who had survived heartbreak and was doing her best to raise her child and move forward with life. Inside, I still carried insecurities that clung tightly to me. The old voices of doubt still whispered: *Are you enough? Will anyone ever love you for who you truly are?*

Instead of silencing those voices with self-love or confidence, I often drowned them out with the same coping mechanisms I had leaned on for years. I chased attention, validation, and the fleeting sense of worth that came from sex. I did not yet know how to see myself as valuable outside of what I could offer physically. I did not yet know how to truly stand in my worth as a woman, mother, and person who deserved love without conditions.

The need for validation took me down another path. It was one that I did not fully recognize at the time as destructive, but which quietly consumed me. It became a craving, an addiction not only to sex, but to pornography and the world of instant gratification it provided. It promised escape, release, and comfort, but in reality, it only deepened the void I was trying so desperately to fill. The more I indulged it, the emptier I felt afterward, as if each moment of false relief dug the hole inside me just a little deeper.

I was not ready yet to embrace the empowered, whole woman I would one day become. I still had to stumble, to struggle, and to confront the darker corners of my story before I could rise into the strength that was waiting for me.

Chapter 3

Chasing Validation

Looking back, I can see so clearly how the foundation of my struggles was laid in my early years. I carried deep insecurity as a child, along with the ache of not quite fitting in and the constant search for approval. Those seeds grew into something much bigger as I entered adolescence and adulthood. What began as feeling overlooked or less than slowly twisted into a desperate hunger to be seen, desired, and feel like I mattered. Somewhere along the way, sex became the language I thought I had to speak to receive love.

It did not happen overnight. It was a slow shaping, a layering of experiences and lies I told myself. Sideways glances and whispered comments became the subtle reinforcement that my worth was linked to how others viewed me. Each glance and comment was like a drop of water carving away at stone, so that by the time I reached adolescence, the groove was already etched deep. I did not consciously decide that sex was my currency. It simply became the language I thought the world required of me.

I did not recognize it at the time, but I was equating attention with worth. The more I was noticed, the more I felt validated, even if that attention was purely physical. By the time I was a teenager, the curve of my body had already begun dictating how people looked at me, how they interacted with me, and in turn, how I measured my own value. It was confusing and intoxicating all at once. I told myself that if men wanted me, then I must matter. That if they looked at me a certain way, if they desired me, then maybe I was not so invisible after all.

Desire is not love. Lust is not safety. Sex, used as a bandage for brokenness, only deepens the wound.

During those years, I could not tell the difference. I remember the way boys' eyes lingered in the hallways at school, the way whispers followed me, how compliments always seemed tangled up with innuendo. On the outside, I laughed it off, pretending confidence. On the inside, I clung to those moments like oxygen. Their words echoed long after the hallways emptied: "You're hot. You're stacked." None of it was love, but it felt like proof that I existed and mattered.

What I did not understand then was how fragile all of it was. I was building my sense of worth on a foundation of sand. Every look, comment, and fleeting moment of desire was unstable ground. It could shift and vanish, and when it did, I was left scrambling to find another glance or word to keep me standing. I was chasing validation like a thirsty runner reaching for water, but the cup was always empty.

I still kept running.

Pornography became an extension of that broken pursuit. At first, it felt like an escape, a way to numb the ache I carried. I would scroll and watch, thinking it was a harmless distraction. It was never just that. It warped my view of intimacy, showing me an impossible version of women, love, and desire. It told me that a woman's value was determined by her body, ability to perform, and willingness to please. Desperate for approval, I tried to live up to it every single day.

I can still remember the first time I stumbled into it. I had not gone intentionally looking for it. It was curiosity mixed with emptiness. What I saw both shocked and fascinated me. I knew it was not real, not in the way life was real, but the images had power. They whispered: *This is what men want. This is what you must be.* Once that seed was planted, it grew rapidly.

What I didn't recognize then was the way pornography distorted my sense of self and understanding of what real love and intimacy was meant to look like. Pornography painted relationships as performance, not presence. It told me that women were supposed to sound, move, and respond in a certain way, as if intimacy were a script rather than a connection. Because I had mentally rehearsed that script so many times, I could never truly be present in the actual moment of sharing myself with another person.

Instead of experiencing the beauty of true connection, I was always performing, comparing, and measuring myself against a false standard that real intimacy could never live up to. When those moments did not feel as dramatic, passionate, or "perfect" as I thought they should, I was left feeling empty, unfulfilled, and convinced that something was wrong with me.

Ironically, the very thing I thought would give me confidence, empowerment, and validation ended up leaving me hollow. I never felt satisfied. I never felt loved. I never felt like I was enough because I was not truly sharing myself. I was giving a performance based on lies I had consumed and internalized.

Even with all the emptiness it brought, I could not break free from the cycle of sexual validation I had created. That need for validation and a desperate hunger to fill the void inside me kept pulling me back. Each moment where I thought I might finally feel whole only deepened my loneliness when the high faded. I thought sex was the answer to everything, that it was the key to being loved, wanted, and valued. In reality, it was a prison of my own making.

I would lie awake after sex, staring at the ceiling, the silence of the night pressing against me. My mind would replay what had just happened, not with satisfaction, but with unease. *Did I do enough? Was I enough? Did they really care about me or just my body?* The validation evaporated as quickly as it came, leaving behind the same gnawing emptiness I had tried so hard to escape.

It was this mindset and desperation for validation that set the stage for the darkest moments of my life. When you confuse attention with love and desire with safety, you put yourself in dangerous places. I did. I opened doors I should have never opened. I ignored red flags because I thought any kind of love, even the kind that hurt me, was better than being unseen. The fear of being invisible was so overwhelming, so suffocating, that my judgment became clouded. I rationalized risky situations, minimized warning signs, and convinced myself that I could somehow control outcomes that were completely beyond my reach. Every "no" I ignored and instinct I pushed aside was like a brick laid on the path toward disaster. I didn't see the weight I was adding until it was too late.

Eventually, my search for validation brought me to a place I could never come back from. The cycle of meaningless sex, warped reality of pornography, and belief that my body was my only offering collided into the brutal reality of being sexually assaulted in my own home. It was violent. It was shattering. Though I had not invited the attack, I carried the weight of shame and self-blame like a second skin. I told myself that I had somehow caused it and that my broken way of thinking had written the script for this nightmare.

Even as my rational mind screamed at me that I was not at fault, my heart and my body betrayed me with whispers of blame, replaying the moments that "led" to it with excruciating detail. Each shadow in my home became suspect, each creak in the floorboard a reminder of my vulnerability. I could no longer sit in silence without feeling the echo of danger.

In the weeks and months that followed, I slipped into a place darker than I had ever known. The emptiness I had carried for years became unbearable, suffocating. I thought about suicide often, convinced that I was beyond repair, that the brokenness inside me was too deep to ever be healed. The days bled into one another, gray and heavy, with laughter feeling distant and hollow. I moved through routines like a ghost, performing the motions of life while inside, a storm raged that no one could see.

Even the smallest tasks-making a meal, folding laundry, smiling at my son felt monumental, requiring an energy I did not have. I remember staring at a sink of dirty dishes as if it were a mountain I could never climb, hearing my son's laughter in the background and feeling the cruel contrast between his joy and my despair. The very thing I had chased-validation, belonging, and love-had left me emptier than ever before.

I did not know it then, but this was only the beginning of a much longer journey. A journey through devastation and despair, through wrestling with shame and survival. A journey that would one day lead me to understanding what true love, worth, and healing really meant.

Though hope felt distant, almost unreachable, there was a flicker. So small I almost did not notice it. But it existed. It was in the brief smile my son gave me when I managed to get out of bed, in the way a kind word from a friend sparked a warmth that did not entirely dissipate. That flicker was fragile, but it was a start.

I remember one afternoon sitting on the edge of my bed, hands limp in my lap, when my son toddled over and pressed his forehead against mine. It was such a small thing, over in seconds, but it pierced the darkness. For the first time in weeks, I felt something other than despair. That flicker whispered that maybe, just maybe, I was not beyond saving.

In this season of my life, all I knew was the darkness. All I knew was the aching lie that sex could make me whole, and the crushing reality that it never would. Every attempt to fill the void left it yawning wider, and each fleeting connection reminded me of what I did not have: safety, acceptance, and unconditional love.

It became increasingly clear that no external source could ever supply the validation I thought I needed. That realization was terrifying, because it meant facing myself. It meant confronting the parts I had hidden, the parts I had denied, the parts I feared most. Even amidst the fear, there was a whisper, a subtle but persistent call to look inward, to begin untangling the mess that had defined my life for far too long. First though, I would have to survive the darkest day of my life.

Chapter 4

When the Darkness Entered

I had always believed that the choices I made-the paths I followed, men I trusted, things I gave of myself-were what defined my story. For so long, I thought I was in control, even when I wasn't. I thought that if I could just be enough-good, sexy, wanted-I could write my own ending. I clung to that illusion of power, convincing myself that I was the one steering my life, even when deep down I knew I was only reacting to my pain.

I told myself that power was in my hands, when in truth it was slipping through my fingers like sand. I thought I could bend circumstances with my will, and if I just pushed hard enough, proved myself enough, I could shape love and life into what I wanted them to be. That illusion gave me comfort, but it was fragile. Beneath it all, I was desperate, clinging to an image of strength while fear quietly steered my choices.

Nothing could have prepared me for the night when control was ripped away from me entirely.

Nothing could have readied me for the way my world would fracture in an instant, for the way safety itself would vanish in a matter of seconds.

He had been watching me for weeks. I didn't know it then, but later the police told me he had been stalking me, studying my routine, waiting for the moment when I was most vulnerable. That knowledge chilled me to my core. To realize that a stranger had been shadowing my life, counting my movements, memorizing my habits, watching without me ever noticing, was its own kind of violation. It meant my home-my sanctuary-had never really been mine. That night, the moment he had been waiting for finally came.

The slider door at the back of my house was open, the screen pulled shut. It was such a small, ordinary thing, something I didn't think twice about. I had walked out of my master bedroom, unaware of the danger lurking just beyond those thin walls. The air was still, the house quiet, and for a split second it felt like any other night. When I turned, everything in me froze.

Standing in my living room was a man I had never seen before, a stranger who had let himself in through the side gate, slipped quietly through my backyard, and stepped into my home as though he belonged there. His presence was wrong, like a nightmare manifesting in the middle of reality.

The room felt warped, stretched thin. Every shadow deepened, every sound magnified. My mind scrambled for explanations, maybe a neighbor, maybe a mistake, but my body already knew the truth. I wasn't safe. The air itself seemed to shift, heavy with threat. One second, my home was familiar. The next, it was foreign, stolen from me in an instant.

The fear that ripped through me in that instant is something words will never fully capture. My body knew before my mind could process it: I wasn't safe. I wasn't in control. What was about to happen was going to change my life forever. My heart pounded in my ears, my legs threatened to give way beneath me, and yet the terror made everything feel hyper focused, his stance, his eyes, the way the silence in the room suddenly felt suffocating.

In seconds, he was on me. I was beaten, overpowered, and raped in my own home. Every moment felt like an eternity. Every second, I begged silently for it to stop, praying under my breath that somehow this wouldn't be the end of my life. Every breath became a fragile thread tethering me to survival, a whispered plea that I might somehow see my son again. The terror was so consuming that I was sure I would never make it through.

Time blurred. Details that should have been forgettable became etched into my memory: the sound of fabric tearing, the metallic taste in my mouth, the way the walls seemed to close in. I counted breaths, not seconds, telling myself to hang on just one more, then another. My prayers weren't eloquent, just desperate fragments whispered inside: "Please. Please. Please." I believed I might never see daylight again.

By the sheer grace of God, I survived. I was not murdered that night. I lived.

Survival doesn't feel like triumph in the immediate aftermath. It feels shaky, disoriented, unreal. Your body breathes, but your soul feels suspended. I remember touching my own skin to confirm I was still there, that I hadn't disappeared into the violence. Survival is a gift, but at that moment, it was also a burden I wasn't sure how to carry.

The aftermath came like waves I couldn't outrun. My body was bruised, my spirit broken, my sense of safety shattered. Even through the fog of fear and pain, one thing was clear: I couldn't let this be hidden. I went to the police immediately. I told them everything. I gave my statement. At the hospital I surrendered my body for evidence, relived the nightmare so it could be recorded in black and white. That was its own kind of violation, necessary, but excruciating. Every question cut me open again. Every detail I spoke aloud made me relive the terror. I had done the right thing, yet it didn't undo the damage inside me.

At the police station, the fluorescent lights were harsh, making everything too sharp and exposed. The sterile smell of gloves and paperwork clung to me. Each question forced me back into the moment I wanted to escape. I remember staring at the officer's pen as it scratched across paper, feeling like my pain had been reduced to lines of ink. Courage didn't feel heroic - it felt like sitting in that chair, answering what I wished I could forget.

Outside of the police, though, almost no one knew. I told only a very small circle, no more than five people. Beyond that, I carried it as a secret, locked inside of me. Not because it hadn't happened, but because I was terrified of what others would say if they knew. I imagined the questions, the looks, the accusations. I imagined people telling me it was my fault, that my choices, past, and body had invited this. The shame was unbearable, and silence felt safer than the possibility of blame.

I walked around with a mask. To the world, I looked like I was surviving. Inside, I was drowning. The truth pressed against my chest like a weight I couldn't lift. Though I had survived that night, I carried a lie that nearly destroyed me in the months that followed: that I deserved what happened to me.

The days after the assault were some of the darkest of my life. I replayed the attack over and over in my head like a film reel I couldn't stop. I jumped at every sound, checked every lock, and still never felt safe. I would lie awake at night, staring at the ceiling, replaying his face, hands, and violence. I felt like a prisoner inside my own skin and home. As much as I fought to stay strong, suicidal thoughts crept in, whispering that maybe leaving this world was the only way to escape the terror that clung to me.

I kept curtains drawn, lights on at odd hours, furniture pushed against doors that were already locked. Still, peace never came. My home had been my sanctuary. Now, it was a cage. Even sleep betrayed me with nightmares that replayed his shadow stepping across my threshold. I lived in a constant state of hyper vigilance, but it didn't bring safety – only deep exhaustion. In that exhaustion, the thought of escape, even permanent escape, seemed like relief.

The deepest wound wasn't just the violence of that night - it was what it did to my sense of worth. Afterward, I couldn't separate myself from what had been done to me. I didn't just feel broken. I felt used. Defiled. Marked. I questioned whether I was lovable or good enough, whether I would ever be more than the body that had been taken from me.

That shame bled into every relationship afterward. I didn't trust men. I didn't trust myself. I felt like intimacy was something dangerous, something that could be ripped away at any moment. Pornography had already clouded my sense of intimacy, but after the assault, the distortion went deeper. Trust felt impossible. Love felt unreachable. Safety felt like a foreign word.

I carried all of this silently. Outwardly, I smiled, I moved forward, I pretended. Inside, I was a battlefield. I blamed myself even though I hadn't done anything wrong. I sought validation in the same places that had always failed me, but now with even less hope they could ever make me feel whole.

Rape didn't just wound my body. It rewired my mind. It convinced me that I was the common denominator in my pain. That no matter what I did, no matter how hard I tried, I would never be enough. When you believe you are unworthy, every choice that follows reflects that belief.

Even in those darkest moments, something inside me refused to give up. Maybe it was God's grace. Maybe it was the tiny voice that whispered that my son needed me. Maybe it was the faint, fragile hope that one day I would not just survive, but live again. Even when I felt buried beneath the rubble of my trauma, there was a spark that refused to be extinguished.

It didn't roar. It glowed like a small and fragile ember, faint but alive. It came in moments as small as my son's hand slipping into mine, as fleeting as the sunrise after another sleepless night. Flickers are enough. They remind you that the darkness isn't absolute.

For a long time, I didn't know how healing would come. I didn't know if it even could, but I was alive, and that meant my story wasn't finished.

Survival came at a cost. The assault didn't just break my body. It rewired my understanding of what safety looked like. Before that night, I believed love was about connection, about being chosen, about proving myself worthy. After that night, love and safety became tangled up in control. I convinced myself that if someone else could take the reins of my life, if they were strong, firm, and dominant enough, then maybe nothing like that would ever happen to me again. Control felt like protection. Submission felt like safety.

When I met the man who would become my second husband, I didn't see the red flags my family saw. They noticed he was much older, headstrong, opinionated, and controlling. To them, he seemed overbearing, a man who wanted things his way and wasn't afraid to make sure it happened. To me, those very traits looked like security. After what I had endured, his dominance felt like a fortress around me. His control promised me I wouldn't have to be the one making choices that could leave me vulnerable.

He was decisive where I was shaky, certain where I was full of doubt. He made rules, and I mistook them for protection. When he ordered food for me at restaurants or spoke over me in conversations, my family bristled. I, however, felt a strange relief, because decisions were no longer mine to make. To me, his authority felt like a shield I could hide behind.

In reality, what I was running toward was not love, but refuge. I didn't understand it then, but trauma had trained me to equate being overpowered with being safe. I thought letting someone else dictate my world meant I would be protected. Instead, it only led me into another kind of prison, one that would take years to fully recognize and begin to break free from.

Chapter 5

The Illusion of Safety

By the time I met him, trauma had already rewritten my definition of safety. I no longer trusted my own instincts or my ability to protect myself. What I wanted was not love. It was relief. I was searching for something solid enough to stand between me and a world that had proven it could shatter me without warning.

Grief does not always announce itself with tears. Sometimes it disguises itself as momentum. You keep moving because stopping feels dangerous. Stillness invites memory. Silence invites truth. I did not feel ready for either. I wanted refuge, not reflection. Protection, not healing. When he entered my life, he seemed to offer exactly that.

He was ten years older than me, a man whose presence seemed magnetic, a mixture of intelligence, charm, and authority. There was an energy about him that drew me in immediately. His voice was calm but commanding, the kind of voice that made you want to listen, trust, and follow. I was fascinated by his stories. He had traveled extensively and seen parts of the world I had not even dreamed of. He spoke with a knowledge and a confidence that made me feel like the universe had finally placed me next to someone who could understand me, who could guide me, who could see me in ways no one else had.

At a time when I felt small and fragile, his presence felt larger than life. He did not just enter a room. He seemed to own it. For a woman who had felt powerless, being near someone who exuded strength felt intoxicating. My bruised spirit mistook that confidence for safety and his dominance for protection.

The connection felt instant, like a spark that ignited a fire I did not know was still capable of burning inside me. My soul seemed to recognize his, and in that recognition, I felt a longing I thought had died along with the naive parts of me. For the first time in a long time, I believed I had met the man of my dreams.

It seemed effortless at first - the way he listened to me, the way he smiled when I spoke, the subtle gestures that made me feel wanted and cherished. It was intoxicating. For someone who had been battered by life and trust, who had learned early that safety was fragile and fleeting, his attention felt like an anchor in a storm. I clung to it, even though a small voice in the back of my mind whispered caution.

That voice was weak, drowned out by the thrill of being seen and the relief of feeling like I had finally found protection. I was searching for refuge, and he offered it in ways I had not known I could crave. His control, certainty, and authority felt like armor I could wrap around myself. After the chaos of what I had endured, the invasion of my home and my body, control felt like salvation. Submission felt like safety.

It did not take long for me to fall deeply, completely, and irreversibly. The first months were a whirlwind of passion, intellectual stimulation, and the illusion of harmony. He could talk about anything. He spoke about books, art, politics, and the nuances of life that had always seemed out of reach in my own small world. He challenged me, made me laugh, and made me feel understood. I felt alive in ways I had not since I was a teenager. I believed with my whole heart that this was the start of forever.

And then a year in, the cracks began to form.

At first, they were subtle. A comment here and a critique there, phrased in ways that made me question myself. "You are overreacting," he would say, as if my feelings were a problem to be managed rather than respected. "You do not understand," as if his perspective was the only one that mattered. I brushed them off. I rationalized and excused and believed that love required patience and compromise. Surely this was just part of knowing each other, I told myself. Surely it would pass.

The comments grew sharper and more frequent. The controlling tendencies became more apparent. He dictated how I should dress, who I should spend time with, and how I should speak and behave. It was subtle at first, a gentle shaping and redirection that felt like guidance. Over time, it became a tightening. It became a cage that I did not realize I was stepping into willingly.

The shift was gradual enough that I barely noticed it. One day it was advice on how to style my hair. Another day, it was criticism of a friend I confided in. Before long, I found myself filtering my words, choosing outfits not based on what I liked but on what would not spark his disapproval. Each concession felt small, insignificant. Together they were bricks building walls around me.

The emotional abuse was insidious. It began to erode my confidence, my self-worth, and my ability to trust myself. I constantly second guessed my thoughts, my choices, and my instincts. If I questioned him, I was met with anger or condescension. If I hesitated, I was told I was weak. If I tried to assert myself, he would turn the situation around and blame me for his anger, his frustration, his control. It was a relentless cycle, one that I did not recognize for what it was because it was masked by moments of affection, of attention, of seemingly genuine love.

Mental abuse came hand in hand with emotional abuse. He was brilliant at twisting reality, at gaslighting, and at making me doubt the truth of my own experiences. If I remembered a conversation one way, he insisted it had happened differently. If I felt hurt by something he did, he told me I was imagining it. Slowly, almost imperceptibly, I began to question myself more than him. My sense of reality, my instincts, the very core of who I was, started to feel fragile.

Physical abuse did not happen immediately, but the tension in the relationship always hinted at its potential. His anger could flare suddenly and unpredictably, and the threat of harm was always present, even if it was veiled in words rather than action. I learned to walk on eggshells, to measure every word, every movement, every expression. I became hyper aware, constantly scanning for danger, constantly assessing how to keep peace in a house that felt more like a battlefield than a home.

The sound of his footsteps in the hallway could change my whole body. I would tense, bracing myself for whether it would be a good night or a bad one. My son's laughter in the other room was often the only thing that reminded me that life still had light in it, even as I lived in shadow.

But the toll of that relationship was not mine alone to bear. My son, though never touched physically, was not untouched by the atmosphere of control that filled our home. He was old enough to notice the way conversations were steered, voices were silenced, and how freedom seemed to shrink when his stepfather was in the room. Children may not always have words for what they sense, but they feel it. They know when space for their thoughts and their laughter is limited. They know when the air is heavy.

I tried to shield him. I kept two worlds running side by side, one a wife and one as my son's mother. It was like living a double life under a single roof. I knew enough to protect a distance, to keep my son out of the line of fire, but protection is not the same as freedom. He could still feel the weight. He could still see me shrink in ways no child should have to see their mother shrink. He learned early what it looked like for a man to dominate a room, decide the tone of every conversation, and strip away the natural freedom a child should have to grow, to stumble, and to simply exist.

Even as I worked to keep those worlds separate, the weight of it pressed deeper into me. It pressed on the most tender part of who I was as a mother. I was haunted by the fear that my son was watching and learning, that he might begin to believe this was what love looked like, that control was strength and dominance was care. I worried that by staying, I was teaching him lessons I never wanted him to carry into his own life, that my silence and endurance might quietly shape the kind of man he would become. The brokenness I already carried only grew heavier as I watched myself remain in a relationship I knew, somewhere deep down, was unhealthy. I told myself it was safe. I tried to believe his control was protection. But in the quiet corners of my mind, I knew better, and that knowledge became its own kind of torment.I asked myself again and again why I could not choose better for my son. Why I wasn't strong enough to walk away. Why I kept convincing myself to stay when every instinct whispered that this was not love. I hated the way I felt split in two, the mother who would protect her child with her life, and the woman who kept clinging to a relationship that stifled her. I knew enough to shield my son from the worst of it, to create distance and maintain those two separate worlds. I also knew that the distance was never enough to erase the atmosphere, and that truth left me with a shame I struggled with daily.

That shame told me I was failing my son. That my brokenness had left me blind, unable to choose what was best for the one person I loved most. Every smile I forced, dinner I prepared, and bedtime story I read was laced with the quiet ache of wondering if I had already let him down beyond repair. The guilt was relentless, a constant reminder that no matter how much I tried to hold my son above the chaos, I still could not silence the storm within me.

I stayed because the control still felt like safety. The armor he wrapped around me and the fortress he projected made me feel protected from the chaos of the outside world. I told myself that the love I felt and the love I craved, required endurance. I told myself that this was a test, a necessary challenge to prove the depth of my commitment. I clung to the illusion that if I could survive him, I could finally find stability, security, and peace.

The first few years were a blur of extremes: intense devotion followed by devastating criticism, moments of passion followed by nights of terror, days of laughter followed by weeks of isolation. I became adept at compartmentalizing and hiding the bruises, both visible and invisible. Friends and family began to notice subtle changes in me, especially my quietness, guardedness, and hesitation. Despite their observation, I could not articulate what was happening. How could I explain that the very person I loved most, the person who had seemed like a savior, had become a source of fear and pain?

I began to lose myself in the relationship, to the point where I no longer recognized the woman I had once been. The traits that had made me unique - my curiosity, warmth, and intellect - were either suppressed or distorted. I constantly molded myself to avoid conflict, earn his approval, and survive another day without angering him. The woman I had been was buried under layers of fear, obligation, and the desperate hope that if I could just get it right, love would prevail.

The worst part was the isolation. He systematically drove a wedge between me and anyone who could see through the illusion. Friends, family, and mentors all became distant as I was pulled deeper into the orbit of his world. Every moment away from him felt like a potential loss. Every interaction outside our relationship was subtly criticized. I became trapped not only by fear, but by the psychological cage he had constructed, one I did not fully recognize until years later.

For fifteen years, I lived in this paradox. The man I had once believed was my soulmate and my refuge was, in truth, my jailer. Every smile, affectionate gesture, and compliment became nothing more than tools to maintain control, hooks designed to keep me tethered. Every harsh word, moment of intimidation, and act of blame was a reminder that I was not safe, that I was not enough, and that I could never meet the impossible standard he demanded. I still kept trying, convincing myself that eventually he would soften, that one day he would finally see me standing there, willing to love him even through his darkness. It was a marathon I ran alone, with no finish line in sight and no victory waiting at the end.

Through it all, I clung to small things. I clung to the good memories I was able to create with my son, the dream that I could one day reclaim myself, and the hope that love could be real. Those fragments of hope were the only things that kept me breathing, the only things that prevented me from believing the nightmare was all there was.

Looking back, I can see the pattern now. I can see the manipulation, gaslighting, and cycle of abuse. Living it was a different reality. I could not leave, not because I did not want to, but because I had been trained to believe that safety lay in submission, that refuge required sacrifice, and that love was something to endure, no matter the cost.

And yet, even in the darkest corners of those fifteen years, there were sparks of clarity. There were moments when I remembered the woman I had been, who had survived assaults, heartbreak, and betrayal. In these moments, I glimpsed the truth: control is never safety, submission is not love, and the person who truly cares for you does not diminish you to elevate themselves.

Those glimpses were small, but they planted seeds which, over time, would grow into awareness, courage, and the strength to break free. These seeds would one day remind me that no matter how long I had been trapped, no matter how convincing the illusion, I was not defined by the cage I had lived in, but by the freedom I would choose to claim.

Chapter 6

Liberation and the Path to Healing

The final years of my marriage were a slow unraveling, a descent that I could feel before I fully understood what was happening. At first, it was subtle, nagging tensions, little arguments that seemed to appear out of nowhere, and a sense of unease that I brushed off as normal marital stress. Underneath it all, something had shifted. The man I had once believed was my anchor, the man whose control had once felt like safety, was no longer a shelter. He was becoming a storm.

It is a terrifying thing to sense the ground beneath your feet give way while still trying to convince yourself that it is steady. That was what the last years of my marriage felt like - an erosion too gradual to name at first, then too undeniable to ignore. I had built so much of my survival on his authority, dominance, and supposed strength, but now those very traits became the weapons that chipped away at my peace.

It started in ways I almost ignored. Prescription pills, he said, were helping him with sleep, stress, and the lingering shadows of his own life. At first, I tried to trust him. After all, he was educated, experienced, and intelligent. I had trusted him for fifteen years - why would I not trust him now? The pills were not just occasional. They became a habit, dependence, and change in the very fabric of his personality.

With the pills came cigarettes. With the cigarettes came alcohol. With the alcohol came rage. It was subtle at first, hidden beneath charm or excuse, but gradually, the veneer cracked. Words turned sharp, insults became attacks, and I began to walk on eggshells, not just to keep the peace, but to survive the unpredictability of his moods. I had been trained by trauma to prioritize safety, but even my instincts were beginning to scream. Something was wrong, and it was far more dangerous than anything I had navigated before.

The physical violence came in waves. Small at first - a shove, a slap, a grab - but then escalated to things I could no longer ignore. I was beaten, pinned, forced into corners, and attacked when he was high. Every incident left me shaken, questioning not only the man I had married but my own choices and capacity to protect myself. I thought, perhaps mistakenly, that love meant endurance, that commitment meant tolerating pain for the sake of stability. But deep inside, I felt the seed of fear growing.

Fear is patient. It begins as a whisper, a hesitation or pause before walking through the door. It then grows into a rhythm in your body, a tightening in your chest, a silent prayer each time you hear footsteps. That was how I lived in those years – I was a woman whose body knew – even before her mind could admit it - that danger was constant, unpredictable, and devastating.

The moment I could no longer deny the danger happened one evening when he was high on prescription medication. Anger flared over a minor disagreement, something trivial and insignificant. His reaction was anything but minor. Words escalated into shoves, and shoves escalated into him strangling me. I struggled, gasping for air, my vision narrowing, panic coursing through my veins. The world dimmed, and then, darkness.

When I woke up, I realized something chilling: I could have died. My body ached, my mind was foggy, but the fear, the raw, primal fear, was unmistakable. The person I had loved - the person I had trusted, who had once seemed like a fortress of protection - had almost ended my life. Even worse, the next day, he did not even remember what had happened. He did not comprehend the gravity of the moment. That was the instant I understood that my life, my very survival, depended on leaving.

I had spent fifteen years enduring control, manipulation, emotional abuse, and physical harm, but nothing had shaken me to the core the way that night did. I realized that love - real, self- respecting love, does not leave you fearing for your life. Safety is not a transaction. Endurance is not a virtue if it comes at the cost of your very being. I knew in that moment that leaving was not just necessary, it was survival.

However, leaving was not simple. For fifteen years, I had been conditioned to bend, excuse, rationalize, and compartmentalize. The thought of leaving stirred every insecurity I had ever carried. *Would I be alone? Could I survive financially? Could I navigate life without the false safety I had clung to for so long?* The answer to all those questions, as painful as it was, became clear: I had to leave, or I might never see another sunrise.

The battle between fear of leaving and fear of staying nearly tore me apart. Both choices carried pain and risk, but only one carried the possibility of life. For the first time in a very long time, I chose myself.

When I finally made the decision to walk away, it was not done in haste but in quiet, deliberate courage. I mapped out my exit one step at a time, not because I lacked resolve, but because trauma had taught me to fear being alone. After years of control and dependence, the idea of standing on my own felt terrifying, so I began slowly.

I separated our sleeping spaces. I learned how to sit with myself in silence without panic. I took small steps toward independence while still telling myself, and him, that I wanted to work on the marriage. Even then, I knew I did not. I was easing myself out of survival mode, loosening the grip of codependency inch by inch, until I could finally stand on my own two feet. Each step was a rebellion against years of conditioning and the lies I had told myself about love and control. And when I finally crossed that threshold, I felt something extraordinary. Relief. The weight that had pressed on me for years, the fear, the anxiety, the constant calculation of how to survive him, was gone. I was free.

Even though I was free, freedom brought its own challenges. I had spent years numbing myself to pain, seeking validation, escape, and refuge in the wrong places. For the first time, I confronted the rawness of my life. The grief, heartbreak, terror, and shame all came rushing in. I could no longer run, mask, or rely on distractions or coping mechanisms. I had to face myself.

It was in that season of confronting truth that I made a vow to myself. For two years, I would live without alcohol, without sex, and without anything that could alter my mind or dull my pain. I would stop numbing. I would stop escaping. I would no longer outrun what hurt.

I chose to sit in the heartbreak and let it wash over me instead of pushing it down. I chose to feel what I had spent years avoiding, to let the grief, fear, and shame surface without interruption. I did not know exactly who I would become on the other side of that decision, but I knew I could not keep living the way I had been.

I committed to facing the wreckage of my past honestly and without anesthesia. Brick by brick. Moment by moment. I would learn how to exist without distraction, without validation, and without surrendering myself to anything that promised relief at the cost of truth.

The first days were the hardest. My body ached for comfort, my mind craved distraction, and my heart desired the illusion of love. I missed the intoxication of control, the thrill of submission, and the twisted comfort of familiarity, even if it had been dangerous. Each day, as I resisted the urge to run back into numbing habits, I felt something shift. My resilience grew. My clarity sharpened. My heart, battered as it was, began to reclaim its own rhythm.

Motherhood also took on a new meaning in this season. For so many years, my son had seen me endure, bend, and try to survive. Now, for the first time, I had the chance to model strength, independence, and healing. I wanted him to see not just a mother who could endure, but a mother who could rise. I wanted him to know that no matter how far brokenness had taken us, we could still choose something better. The thought of him gave me courage on the hardest days. He deserved a mother who fought for her life, and I was determined to be that example.

I threw myself into self-reflection, therapy, meditation, journaling, and every method I could find to reconnect with the woman I had been before fear and abuse dictated my life. I allowed myself to cry until the tears ran dry, to scream until my lungs burned, to sit in silence until I could hear the whispers of my own soul again. I did not rush the process. I honored the pain. I honored the heartbreak. Slowly, painstakingly, I began to feel the first glimmers of healing.

The mornings became sacred. I would wake up, pour a cup of coffee, and sit in the quiet of my home, listening to the world waking up outside. Each breath, each sip, was an act of grounding, a way to remind myself that I was alive, that I was still here, that I had survived. Walking through the house, untouched by fear for the first time in years, was a revelation. Every step, glance, and room became a testament to my liberation. My home no longer felt like a prison. It was mine again, and that alone was healing.

Afternoons were spent in introspection and creativity. I wrote pages in my journal, sometimes spilling tears onto the paper, sometimes scribbling ideas that had been buried for years. I read books about trauma, healing, and self-empowerment. I meditated, often sitting for hours, facing the silence, memories, and myself without flinching. These hours were not easy - they were excruciating - but they were the foundation of my rebirth.

Evenings brought reflection and patience. I learned to be alone without feeling lonely. I learned to confront my cravings for escape and denial, to recognize them as illusions rather than needs. I began to notice the subtle changes in my body and mind: calmer breaths, steadier hands, and a sense of clarity that had been absent for years. I started walking outside, feeling the sun on my face, wind on my skin, and earth beneath my feet. Each step reminded me that life continued, healing was happening, and I could rebuild my sense of safety and self.

I also confronted my relationship patterns and the ways I had allowed manipulation and control to dictate my choices. I reflected on the red flags I had ignored, signs I had rationalized, and fears I had coddled. Slowly, I recognized the ways trauma had wired me to accept abuse as safety. With this recognition came freedom, a growing awareness that I could choose differently next time. I could set boundaries, demand respect, and protect myself without fear or shame.

Two years of intentional abstinence, total sobriety, and complete self-honesty became a sanctuary. I built a relationship with myself that was untouchable, unshakeable, and profound. For the first time in years, I experienced a sense of empowerment that was not tied to another person's validation, approval, or presence. I was whole because I chose to be, because I had survived, and because I refused to run from the pain that had once consumed me.

I faced the heartbreak fully. I mourned the loss of the life I thought I had, the illusions of love I had believed in, and the years I had spent living under fear and manipulation. In mourning, I found clarity. In acknowledging the pain, I found strength. In committing to my own growth, I found hope.

Looking back, leaving was not just an act of courage. It was an act of reclamation. I took back everything that had been stolen from me: my safety, voice, power, and dignity. In the process, I discovered a truth that had been obscured by trauma for far too long: I could endure heartbreak without escaping. I could confront pain without numbing. I could survive without surrendering my soul.

The journey was not easy, and the shadows of the past did not vanish overnight. However, I had discovered a powerful, transformative principle: healing is intentional. Survival is a choice. Liberation, true liberation, begins when you refuse to allow fear, abuse, or manipulation to dictate the terms of your life.

By the end of those two years, I was not just surviving. I was thriving in a way I had never known. I had confronted the darkest chapters of my life, and instead of burying them or allowing them to define me, I had used them as a crucible to forge a stronger, wiser, and more resilient self. I had discovered that true safety does not come from control, submission, or reliance on another. It comes from within.

And as I stood in that truth, I realized something profound: liberation is not an event. It is a process. It is a series of choices, each one reinforcing the courage, clarity, and power that had always existed inside me. Once I claimed that liberation, there was no going back. I was free.

Chapter 7

Reclaiming Myself

Walking out of that marriage was like stepping off a cliff without knowing if I could fly. For years, I had been tethered to a man whose control felt like safety, whose love was coated in manipulation, whose presence masked danger. Leaving him was not just a choice. It was a declaration of life, survival, and a reclamation everything that had been eroded inside me.

The first nights alone were disorienting. I remember lying in my quiet apartment, the familiar hum of the refrigerator, the soft creak of the floorboards, and the emptiness around me pressing in like a physical weight. My mind had been running on autopilot for years, surviving, anticipating, and performing. Now, the silence was deafening. It forced me to confront the raw truth of who I was without someone else's influence shaping my every thought and action.

There were nights when I stared at the ceiling for hours, retracing the years I had lost, the compromises I had made, the bruises, both visible and invisible, that I carried like secret tattoos on my soul. I could hear the echo of old arguments in the quiet, like they had been imprinted into my body. At first, that silence felt unbearable, like being trapped in a room with ghosts. Slowly, as the weeks went on, I realized that silence was not empty. It was space. It was an opportunity. It was the place where healing could begin.

I committed, from the very beginning, to total sobriety. No alcohol, no numbing distractions, no sex to fill the emptiness or blur the pain. The first weeks were brutal. Every night, memories of the past, abuse, betrayal, and mistakes, rushed in with relentless intensity. I had to face myself in ways I had avoided for years. I had to sit with grief, with shame, and with fear, without running. The temptation to escape, to soften the edges with distractions, was strong, but I resisted.

In that resistance, I learned how powerful presence really is. When you strip away the anesthetics - the wine at the end of a hard day, casual sex, mind-numbing scrolling - you are left with yourself. Just you. For most of us, that is the scariest place to be. For me, it became the beginning of something holy, something life giving.

This intentional pause gave me clarity. Abstaining from sex allowed me to disentangle desire from validation, intimacy from performance. I realized how much of my adult life had been shaped by external expectations. I had spent years bending to fit what others wanted me to be, whether it was a partner, a friend, or society's idea of a "successful woman." Now, free from external pressures, I could ask myself the simplest, hardest questions: *Who am I when no one is watching? What do I truly enjoy? What makes me feel alive?*

Some days, I sat with those questions for hours, pen in hand, journaling until the ink smudged beneath my tears. Other days, I did not have answers. I only had the ache. Over time, the answers began to take shape. I discovered a woman I had not fully known. She was sharp minded, fiercely intelligent, creative, ambitious, and capable of extraordinary focus. I realized I had talents I had never allowed myself to fully explore because I was busy surviving or molding myself for someone else. I was good at business. I was good at real estate. I was good at construction. These were not just skills. They were lifelines to autonomy, evidence of competence, and proof that I could build my life on my own terms.

Within a few months, I became a licensed realtor and a licensed general contractor. I started businesses, built them from the ground up, and sold them successfully. Each contract signed, each property renovated, and each deal closed was a tangible reminder of my agency. For the first time in years, I felt a kind of validation that came from myself, not from the dangerous mirror of someone else's approval. I was finally seeing what I was capable of when I trusted my own mind and instincts.

Even with financial independence and professional success, the hollow emptiness lingered. Money could buy freedom, stability, and comfort, but it could not buy fulfillment, peace, or a healed heart. I could fill my home with everything I had dreamed of, yet the quiet corners of my soul still echoed with loneliness and unresolved pain. Achievement became both a soothing balm and a sharp reminder that external victories alone could never reach the depths of healing I truly needed.

The deeper work came in the solitude I allowed myself. I journaled obsessively, pouring out fears, memories, grief, and victories onto paper. I reflected on my patterns with relationships, intimacy, and self-worth. I asked hard questions: *What have I been running from? Why did I compromise myself? What parts of me have I ignored or hidden to survive?* The answers were not easy, and sometimes the pain was almost unbearable, but the act of facing it all without numbing it became an essential part of my transformation.

Through sobriety and self-reflection, I began to untangle my desires from the layers of conditioning imposed by past partners. I realized that for years, I had been performing in relationships, molding myself to fit someone else's fantasy rather than honoring my own needs. I had given pieces of myself away for approval, safety, and fleeting validation. Now, I could feel my own pleasure, power, and choice. This was not selfishness. It was a reclamation. It was learning that the woman I had been suppressing could exist fully and unapologetically.

This process extended into every part of my life. Professionally, I thrived because I was no longer afraid to assert myself. I negotiated deals, took calculated risks, and made decisions with confidence rather than fear. My success was no longer performative. It was real, grounded in competence and clarity. Every business I launched, every property I developed, and every client relationship I nurtured became a reflection of my regained autonomy and focus.

Financial achievements were exhilarating, but more importantly, they allowed me to reclaim my sense of self. For years, I had measured worth through the eyes of others, through the lens of approval and attention. Now, I measured worth by results, effort, and integrity. Success became a mirror reflecting my own resilience, capacity to thrive, and ability to create stability from chaos.

Even in my personal life, sobriety allowed me to rebuild trust in myself. I had lived for so long in a state of hypervigilance, conditioned by abuse and control, that trusting my instincts felt foreign. Each decision I made, from negotiating a contract to choosing how to spend my evenings, was an affirmation: I am capable. I am safe. I can navigate life on my own terms.

Those choices were not always dramatic. Sometimes it was as simple as choosing solitude over company that drained me. Sometimes it was saying no without apology. Sometimes it was cooking myself a meal and enjoying it without guilt, without rushing. These small choices stacked together became a new rhythm for my life, a rhythm built on dignity and self-respect instead of fear and people pleasing.

I also learned to recognize and dismantle unhealthy patterns I had carried for years. I noticed how often I defaulted to pleasing others, compromising my values, or silencing my own needs to maintain approval. Through therapy, reflection, and discipline, I began to set boundaries without apology. That looked like saying no when something felt wrong, even if it disappointed someone. It meant ending conversations when my truth was being dismissed instead of arguing to be understood. It meant honoring my instincts rather than explaining them away.

I learned to assert myself without anger and without fear, to speak plainly about what I would and would not tolerate, and to walk away from situations that required me to abandon myself to keep the peace.

Honoring my truth was no longer about confrontation. It was about alignment. I was no longer negotiating my worth. I was protecting it. In doing so, I wasn't just cultivating self respect. I was building an unshakeable foundation for the life I wanted to live.

The process was not linear. Some days, the emptiness returned with a sharp intensity, a reminder that trauma leaves traces that achievement and independence alone cannot erase. Memories of past abuse, fear of being unseen, and echoes of self-doubt would surface, uninvited and raw. Each time, I faced them with tools I had developed: self-compassion, reflection, and accountability. Every encounter with old pain strengthened my resilience and deepened my understanding of myself.

I also found solace and power in small rituals. Morning walks, journaling, and quiet reflection became daily acts of presence and gratitude. I learned to celebrate my victories alone, without needing anyone else to witness or approve them. I discovered joy in being fully present in my own life, immersed in creation, strategy, and problem solving, not performing for anyone else's gaze.

Sometimes it was as simple as sitting outside with a cup of coffee, watching the sun rise, and feeling the air shift as the world woke up around me. Other days it was cooking a meal just for myself, plating it with care, and realizing that I was worthy of nourishment, not just survival. These small acts of honoring myself stitched together the larger truth: healing happens in the ordinary as much as in the extraordinary.

By the end of my second year out of the marriage, I was transformed. I was financially independent, professionally accomplished, emotionally more self-aware, and deeply in touch with myself, I had begun to experience life on my own terms. I could navigate challenges without fear, celebrate success without needing validation, and enjoy intimacy and connection as choices, not lifelines. I had built a life that reflected my true self, not a version molded to meet someone else's expectations.

This transformation was not mine alone. My son noticed the shift too. He saw the way I carried myself differently, the way laughter returned to our home, the way I no longer walked on eggshells. He may not have understood every detail, but he could feel the difference between the shadowed mother who had been surviving and the lighter mother who was finally living. In reclaiming myself, I was also giving him a gift: a living picture of resilience, proof that healing is possible, and a home where love could breathe again.

Even with all this clarity and accomplishment, I knew healing was ongoing. True fulfillment was not a destination. It was a daily practice of presence, self-trust, and intentionality. I had learned that no amount of success could replace the work of feeling, processing, and integrating trauma. Real healing required embracing vulnerability, confronting fear, and cultivating a life aligned with values rather than validation.

Walking away from that marriage had been the hardest, most terrifying act of my life, but it was also the most liberating. I had reclaimed my body, my mind, my decisions, and my future. I had discovered that the person I had always been capable of becoming - a woman grounded, strong, intelligent, and self-aware - was finally emerging. Even though there were shadows of doubt, fear, and grief, I had the tools, insight, and strength to face them without surrendering my power.

The journey was not about proving myself to anyone else. It was about proving to myself that I could survive, rebuild, and thrive. It was about learning that joy, fulfillment, and love could be chosen, not demanded, earned, or performed. It was about understanding that my worth was inherent, not contingent on others' approval, attention, or control.

As I looked ahead, I realized something profound: freedom, clarity, and true empowerment are not gifts given. They are reclaimed. They are claimed in the moments when you refuse to numb, when you sit with pain rather than running, and when you choose yourself even when it is terrifying.

Choosing yourself is not an abandonment of others. It is the reclamation of everything you were created to be. It is a daily act of courage, a steady refusal to shrink, and a promise to the woman staring back at you in the mirror that she is worth the fight. What I didn't yet realize was that reclaiming myself was only the beginning. This compass I had found would soon expand by a force much greater than myself. My life was about to shift in ways that no amount of discipline or self-awareness could have prepared me for.

Chapter 8

The Moment God Became Real

Even though I had lived years devoted to self-help, personal growth, and mastering my own mind, I had no desire or reason to acknowledge the presence of God in my life. I had spent countless hours reading Wayne Dyer, Tony Robbins, Marianne Williamson, and others. I had built a framework of understanding that said the universe, your life, and your destiny are shaped entirely by your own effort, reflection, and dedication. We are our own eternal power. Anything is achievable if we are willing to grow, to confront ourselves, to continue evolving as human beings. I believed that. I had invested myself in that mindset completely. I believed in the power of human potential, in the ability to rise above circumstances, in the notion that every obstacle could be overcome with focus, discipline, and self-awareness. I had created a life philosophy that left little room for miracles, little room for the unseen, little room for anything that could not be rationalized, analyzed, or explained.

It was in the quiet darkness of my bedroom, kneeling on the floor in a state of clarity and presence that came only from years of sobriety and abstinence, that He found me.

It started with a voice. Not a whisper, not a distant echo, but a voice so clear, so vivid, that it startled me awake from a deep sleep. I felt a presence descend upon me, pulling me gently yet powerfully to my knees. My heart raced with an anxiety I could not place, yet at the same time, a deep calm settled in my chest, wrapping around me like a blanket. The voice called my name.

"What?" I said, almost laughing nervously because it didn't feel real.

"I am your Lord. I am your God," came the response, unmistakable and profound.

I laughed again, a nervous, disbelieving chuckle. Surely this could not be real. I had spent my life avoiding religion because of the hypocrisy and judgment I had witnessed. I had long believed that people used God to justify cruelty, to control others, or to point fingers at faults rather than to surrender themselves to truth and transformation. I had seen faith weaponized instead of lived, used to dominate rather than to heal. I had witnessed so much pain, manipulation, and brokenness from people claiming to serve God that I had hardened myself to the possibility of genuine spiritual connection. And yet, here there was a voice, undeniable, claiming to be the source of everything, speaking directly to me.

I felt a whirlwind of emotions: disbelief, awe, fear, love, safety, and vulnerability all at once. I was overwhelmed, completely unprepared for the weight and beauty of what was happening. Amidst the anxiety, there was also clarity. I knew, deep in my bones, that this presence was real. I could feel it. I could hear it. I could not deny it, no matter how hard I tried.

He told me I was His. That He loved me. That He had been trying to reach me for a long time, patiently waiting for a moment when I was fully awake, fully present, fully myself. And then came the words that shifted everything: "If you are willing to listen, I will be present for every moment of your life moving forward."

At first, I did not fully understand what it meant. I had been conditioned to rely on myself, to trust only my own mind, my own work, my own discipline. To think that an external presence could walk with me through life, unseen yet deeply real, challenged every assumption I had ever made about reality. I had spent decades believing that independence and self-reliance were the ultimate virtues, that vulnerability was weakness, and that asking for help was a failure. Now, I was confronted with the reality that there was an intelligent, loving, and omnipresent God that not only cared for me, but had been waiting patiently for me to truly see Him.

The proof was undeniable. I could feel it in the way my body responded, how my chest expanded, how my mind quieted, and how every corner of fear and doubt softened just enough to let me breathe. I felt love in a form I had never experienced: unconditional, unwavering, protective, intimate in a way that transcended physicality or human relationships. For the first time in my life, I felt fully held. Fully accepted. Fully known. Every atom in my body resonated with the presence. The sensation was at once electrifying and grounding, a paradox I could not fully explain. It was as if every molecule of my being had been waiting for this touch of recognition, this affirmation that I was not alone in my struggles, fears, and joys.

In that moment, I realized that my years of self-help, personal discipline, and growth had not been wasted. They had prepared me for this. They had brought me to a place of vulnerability and presence where I could recognize Him, hear Him, and respond to Him. Without sobriety, self-reflection, and the years of painstaking work on myself, I may have brushed it off as imagination, sleep paralysis, or wishful thinking. But I was ready, and I knew it.

Tears streamed down my face as I processed it. The weight of my disbelief, the skepticism I had carried my entire life, melted into a pure, awestruck recognition. I had never experienced anything like it: the simultaneous combination of vulnerability and security, fear and trust, anxiety and peace. It was magical. It was terrifying. It was life altering. I could feel the air in the room charged with a presence that defied explanation, yet it was tangible in every sense of the word. Every heartbeat, every breath, every blink became a dialogue with something greater than myself.

For years, I had carried pain, shame, fear, and the weight of my past mistakes. But in this moment, I felt seen in a way that transcended human judgment or societal expectations. I was not my past. I was not defined by what I had done or what had been done to me. I was fully loved and fully known. There was a profound sense of worth instilled in me, one that no human validation could ever replicate.

As the night unfolded, I remained on my knees, talking quietly in my mind, listening intently, asking questions that had lived in the corners of my consciousness for years. He responded, not with complexity, not with doctrine, not with judgment, but with clarity and guidance. Every word, every feeling, every moment of presence reinforced the reality of His existence and the depth of His care. I felt my soul expanding, stretching into a space I did not even know existed. I could feel my emotional armor cracking, releasing grief, pain, and fear that had been lodged there for decades. Each release was accompanied by a deep, almost euphoric sense of freedom.

I remember thinking about my life - the abuse, pain, loss, years of striving and self-discipline - and suddenly, all of it made sense in a new way. My past was not to be viewed as punishment or failure, but as the preparation and foundation for a new chapter. For the first time, I could see my life not as a series of mistakes or burdens, but as a narrative that had brought me to this profound point of awakening. Each trauma, heartbreak, and moment of striving had been leading me to this divine encounter.

It was also a moment of challenge. The voice made it clear that I was not to seek Him as a crutch, nor was I to hand over my agency blindly. I was to continue my work in the world, to continue my reflection, growth, and discipline, but now with guidance, not just effort. With presence, not just self-reliance. With love, not just striving. I understood that true partnership with God required awareness, humility, and trust, not passive surrender.

In the following days and weeks, the experience stayed with me. I felt a subtle, constant awareness of Him in my life. It was not a sensory hallucination, nor a passing feeling, it was a new baseline for existence. I began noticing patterns, coincidences, moments of intuition that I could not explain, moments where I knew

I was not alone. Every decision, every reflection, every challenge carried a whisper of guidance, a sense of being held, a deep knowing that I was not facing life by myself.

I also realized that this experience could not be reduced to religion or doctrine. It was not about dogma, not about judgment, not about rituals. It was about relationships, presence, and connection. It was about truth that transcended human understanding, about a love that is unconditional and infinite, about a guidance that does not demand perfection but simply presence. It was a deeply personal awakening that anyone, from any walk of life, could recognize as transformative, without having to subscribe to organized religion.

Even in moments of doubt or struggle, the memory of that night - the clarity, voice, love, and presence - all remained an anchor. It was a touchstone I could return to, a grounding in the midst of chaos. For the first time, I could navigate life with a sense of partnership, not just discipline. I could face fear with reassurance. I could confront pain with perspective. I could move forward knowing that I was not only capable of thriving, but worthy of being loved, guided, and seen in my entirety.

This moment did not erase the challenges, the pain, or the mistakes of my life. It did not suddenly transform me into someone immune to hardship or grief. However, it gave me a compass, an anchor, and the unshakable truth that I was not walking alone.

In the weeks and months that followed, I began to realize how much that night had altered the very framework of my life. Nothing external had changed. My work was still demanding, my responsibilities were still present, and my memories of pain still lingered. However, the lens through which I experienced all of it had shifted.

Morning felt different. Where I once woke with a sense of heaviness or dread, I now carried a quiet awareness that I was not waking alone. My mornings began with small prayers whispered before my feet touched the floor, not scripted or memorized, but raw and personal: "Be with me today. Guide me. Show me how to walk this path." Even when I did not feel particularly holy or spiritual, those words grounded me.

At work, I noticed subtle shifts in how I carried myself. I had always been disciplined and sharp, but now I approached decisions with a new layer of peace. Before, every mistake felt like a threat to my worth, every failure a verdict. Now, I began to trust that even setbacks could hold purpose, that they might carry lessons I could not see in the moment. My confidence no longer came only from competence. It came from knowing I was not navigating the world alone.

Relationships, too, began to look different. Where I once approached people guardedly, with layers of armor built from betrayal and disappointment, I found myself softening, just a little at a time. I could listen without the same level of defensiveness. I could extend grace where once I would have snapped in judgment. Though I was not ready to throw myself into deep intimacy again, I could feel the soil of my heart being tilled, prepared for something healthier, something rooted in truth rather than fear.

This new awareness was not without struggle. Doubt crept in at unexpected times. I would be driving down the highway or washing dishes at the sink, and suddenly the memory of that night felt distant, like maybe it had all been in my head. The voice of skepticism, the same one that had guarded me for decades, whispered, "You imagined it. You wanted to believe so badly that you created it." Those moments were agonizing because the last thing I wanted was to be deceiving myself.

Every time the doubt grew loud, something quiet and unmistakable broke through. A feeling, a whisper of reassurance, a perfectly timed coincidence that brought peace. It was not dramatic, but it was consistent. A friend would call with words I needed to hear. A passage I stumbled across in a book would speak directly to what I was wrestling with. A moment of intuition would lead me to make a choice that turned out to be exactly right. Again and again, I was reminded: this was not imagination. This was a relationship.

I also noticed how His presence began to shape the way I saw my past. Instead of replaying memories as proof of my brokenness, I began to see them as chapters of a larger story that had prepared me for this very awakening. The abuse, mistakes, and years of striving were no longer just scars. They were part of the map that had led me here. This realization softened something inside me. I began to forgive myself more easily. I began to hold my younger self with compassion rather than contempt.

Even the quiet moments alone in my apartment shifted. Silence had once been suffocating, pressing in with the weight of loneliness. Now, silence became sacred. I would sit on the floor with a journal, or sometimes simply sit with nothing but my breath, and feel Him there. Sometimes I spoke aloud, sometimes I cried, sometimes I just let the stillness wash over me. For the first time, I realized solitude did not have to equal emptiness - it could be communion.

Of course, this did not mean life suddenly became easy. There were still days when fear tried to pull me under, when old triggers resurfaced, when the ache of my story felt unbearable. Even on those days, the memory of that night remained like a flame that could not be extinguished. A reminder that even when I could not feel Him, He was still there. The love I had experienced was not a fleeting dream, but an unshakable truth. What started as a single night of undeniable presence became the foundation for a new way of living. It wasn't just a single event experience to be fondly remembered but a reality that I had to walk out every single day.

Chapter 9

Life After Awakening

The moment God made Himself undeniably real in my life didn't just shift my understanding of the universe. It shifted me. It shifted how I understood myself, my purpose, and my relationships with every single person around me. After thirty-six years of living inside the frameworks of self-help, personal discipline, and self-reliance, I was now faced with a new reality: I could no longer rely solely on myself. I should not rely solely on myself. I was being invited into a partnership far greater than I had ever imagined, and it required surrender. Not of my agency, but of the illusion that I could carry life alone.

This new awareness brought both exhilaration and uncertainty. On one hand, it was profoundly liberating. I had spent decades measuring myself against standards that weren't my own, pushing to grow, reflect, and excel, but often feeling an emptiness that no amount of achievement, recognition, or success could fill. I now understood why. I had been living in a partial reality. My efforts were noble, but incomplete. I had been trying to build a life, a sense of self, and a path forward without acknowledging the God's presence that could guide me through it all.

On the other hand, this awakening was deeply disorienting. How do you take a life lived in self-reliance, in the pure logic of effort and discipline, and suddenly open it to something you cannot fully see or control? How do you navigate the world when your internal compass is no longer just your intellect, your experience, or your instinct, but also the guidance of a presence that is immeasurably vast, unfathomably wise, and entirely personal?

I spent the first six months after that moment almost entirely in private. I couldn't yet share this experience with anyone. Words like God, Jesus, Spirit, or presence felt foreign, vulnerable, and dangerous. I feared judgment, misunderstanding, and ridicule. I had friends, colleagues, family, but I didn't know how to explain what had happened. Even the thought of casually saying God spoke to me in conversation made my chest tighten. I felt like my internal reality had expanded into a dimension that no one else could yet perceive.

During those months, I explored churches. I searched for a place that felt genuine, that didn't feel rigid, judgmental, or performative. I wasn't looking for people to tell me what to believe. I was looking for a space to continue learning, to grow in understanding, to study the Bible in a way that helped me make sense of what had just occurred. I needed a foundation for the truth I had experienced. I needed context. I needed language that matched the reality I could no longer ignore.

Finding that space was not simple. Many churches and communities came with rules I didn't understand, expectations I couldn't meet, or beliefs that seemed rigid or exclusionary. I walked into Sunday services feeling simultaneously exhilarated and alienated—thrilled that a community could exist for people seeking God, yet hesitant to admit to anyone what I had experienced. I had been changed internally and eternally, but my external reality hadn't yet caught up with my internal shift. I was a woman transformed, but still inhabiting the same world, same job, same friends, same routines.

This gap created tension. I couldn't speak openly about what I was experiencing, but I couldn't pretend it wasn't there. Every conversation, every interaction, every moment of solitude reminded me that my life had changed fundamentally. I started journaling obsessively, writing out thoughts, prayers, questions, doubts, fears, and reflections. These pages became a sacred space, a laboratory for understanding the new self I was becoming. The act of writing was meditative, almost holy. Each word was a step closer to clarity, a gentle untangling of the mind from old habits and the opening of space for something greater.

One of the biggest shifts was in my understanding of purpose. For decades, I had pursued personal growth, financial success, and professional achievement as if they were ends in themselves. While I had accomplished so much, I had felt an emptiness that these milestones could never fill. Now, I understand why. My purpose was not about achievement alone. It was about living intentionally, using the gifts and talents I had cultivated to serve others and honor the life I had been given. Every business decision, professional move, and personal choice now carried a deeper meaning. It wasn't about what I could get. It was about what I could give, how I could make an impact, and how I could honor the God, who had transformed me.

Dating became a question I hadn't anticipated. How do you approach love when your framework has shifted so drastically? I had spent so long measuring relationships by what I could receive, what attention I could command, and what validation I could secure, but now I wanted something completely different. I wanted a connection that honored my newfound identity, my commitment to abstinence, and my desire for a partnership that was authentic, grounded, and purposeful. I wanted to meet someone not to fill a void, but to share a life in alignment with the principles I now embraced.

I had no roadmap. My friends, most of them, didn't understand. Some were still living in worlds where casual dating and immediate gratification were the norm. Conversations about God, purpose, or intentional living often ended with awkward pauses, polite nods, or quick subject changes. Despite this, I knew I couldn't compromise my truth. I couldn't go back to my old ways. I couldn't pretend that the internal shift hadn't occurred. There was a loneliness in this realization, a quiet isolation that came with being ahead of my environment in understanding myself and my purpose. It was also exhilarating, like standing on the edge of something vast, knowing that the leap would redefine my life.

Friendships, too, required recalibration. I began to notice the ways in which relationships had been transactional or conditional in my life. Some friends thrived on gossip, competition, or comparison. Others sought validation or support only when it suited them. I realized I no longer wanted relationships built on those foundations. I wanted connections that were authentic, nurturing, and mutually uplifting. I wanted people who could witness my growth, respect my boundaries, and honor the journey I was on. Slowly, I began to identify who could walk this new path with me, and who could not. It was difficult, but necessary, to protect the space I had created for growth.

The process of redefining relationships wasn't immediate. I spent many months navigating awkwardness, testing conversations, setting boundaries, and sometimes distancing myself from people I loved but could no longer engage with authentically. I learned the importance of patience, not just with others, but with myself. I couldn't expect the world to immediately adjust to the woman I was becoming, and I couldn't force myself into old patterns for the sake of comfort or familiarity. Each decision, each boundary, each conversation became a practice in discernment, teaching me to honor my own needs while remaining open to love, connection, and guidance.

In the midst of all this, my faith deepened, not as a set of rules or obligations, but as a living, breathing partnership. I began to notice subtle ways in which guidance showed up in my daily life. Decisions felt clearer. Challenges felt surmountable. I felt supported in ways I had never experienced before. I began to pray, not as a ritual, not as an obligation, but as a conversation. I began to sense an active, listening presence that was invested in my growth, my choices, and my joy. Prayer became a dialogue, a lifeline, a mirror of my own heart reflecting the love and guidance I could trust.

As my faith deepened, so did a quiet calling to pour into others, particularly young women standing at the same crossroads I once stood at without guidance. I felt a deep burden for girls in high school and those just stepping into adulthood, an age where identity feels fragile and the world is loud with expectations. I saw how easily young women learn to measure their worth through attention, relationships, and approval, often letting someone else define who they are before they ever have the chance to know themselves.

I began mentoring them not as an expert, but as someone who had lived the consequences of losing herself too early. I wanted them to understand that their value was not something to be earned, performed, or affirmed by a man, but something already established by God. These conversations were not about rules or perfection. They were about truth, discernment, boundaries, and learning how to listen for a voice greater than the noise of the world. In guiding them toward Christ, I was reminded again and again that healing multiplies when it is shared, and that purpose often reveals itself not through ambition, but through service. In those moments, sitting across from young women and speaking truth into places I once felt lost myself, I felt a kind of fulfillment I had never found in achievement alone. It was quieter than success, less visible, but deeper. It settled in my chest instead of my ego.

The first year after my awakening was the most challenging and transformative of my life. I was learning to navigate the world with a new heart, perspective, and framework for living. Every day was a test of trust, patience, and courage. There were moments of doubt, when old habits tempted me, when fear or insecurity whispered that I was too different, too alienated, too vulnerable. In those moments, I learned to pause, to pray, to reflect, and to realign. I was discovering a rhythm of life that balanced presence, discernment, and courage.

There were also unexpected blessings. I began to see beauty in places I had once overlooked. A quiet morning walk felt like communion. A conversation with a stranger carried a spark of divine timing. A difficult challenge at work revealed itself as an opportunity for growth and trust. Life was no longer random. It was patterned, woven, orchestrated with a care that I had never before recognized. Even the pain had meaning. Even the struggles carried lessons. Even the silences were filled with presence.

By the end of that year, I realized that my life had entered a new dimension. I was no longer living solely in the logic of effort, the calculations of achievement, or the constant striving for external validation. I was living in partnership with a God that was loving, wise, and constant. I was living with purpose, with intent, with clarity. I was beginning to understand that this partnership was not passive. It required engagement, reflection, and courage to act in alignment with truth.

The challenge, of course, was to integrate this transformation into every aspect of my life. To live authentically while still interacting with a world that often didn't share my vision. To date with intention, to befriend with discernment, to work with purpose, to spend time in reflection, and to honor both the visible and invisible dimensions of my life. Each decision became layered: *How does this choice align with my values? How does it serve my purpose? How does it honor the presence guiding me? How does it honor the life I have been given?*

In 2018, as I stepped into this new reality, I realized that my life had been preparing me for this moment for decades. Every heartbreak, every period of self-doubt, every success and failure had led to this awakening. And now, living in the aftermath, I understood that the work of life was not about perfection, but about alignment, intention, and connection with self, with others, and with the presence that had transformed me.

I was no longer a woman seeking to fill voids with external validation. I was no longer a woman defining herself through performance, achievement, or approval. I was a woman in partnership with something greater, navigating life with intentionality, courage, and love. That reality is both exhilarating and terrifying, but was also just the beginning.

Chapter 10

Living Love Story

When I look back at that first year after encountering God, I see it as a love story, one unlike anything I had ever imagined or even thought possible. It was not the kind of love story that ends in heartbreak or demands conditions. It was not a fragile thing that depended on my performance or my worthiness. It was an unshakable, steady presence that said, "You are mine. You are loved. You were created with purpose."

For the first time since I was a little girl, I was living without anxiety. For the first time since I was eight years old, I did not wake up with the heavy knot of tension sitting in my chest. Instead, I woke up to mornings that felt light, open, and purposeful. I felt seen. I felt held. Most of all, I felt as though my life mattered, not in the shallow sense of being noticed or admired by other people, but in the eternal sense of belonging to something greater than myself.

That awareness shifted everything. It shifted the way I looked at myself, the way I approached relationships, and even the way I moved through the simplest details of everyday life. I could not hide it anymore - not from my family or friends, and certainly not from myself. It was impossible to encounter the living God and then try to tuck Him away like some private secret. My entire being had been rearranged, and it started spilling out of me whether I wanted it to or not.

I began speaking, carefully at first, about what was happening in my life. I shared bits of my story in small group settings, opening myself in ways that scared me. I began searching more deeply for community. I visited churches, one after another, until I finally found one that felt like home. It wasn't about performance or perfection. It was about creating space for growth, questions, and faith in practice. It was there that I began learning not only about the Bible as a historical and spiritual text, but about who Jesus truly is and how God designed creation with such breathtaking detail and purpose.

Something else began shifting in that season. My focus turned outward. For thirty-six years, my eyes had been locked inward, on my own pain, striving, self-help pursuits, anxieties, and ambitions. Even my attempts to "become better" through self-help were ultimately about me. Now, my life began to open up in a new direction. I wanted to live for people instead of myself.

That was not a casual decision. It was the result of dying to my ego, of laying down the pride that had told me my strength alone could get me through life. In that death, I discovered a new birth. I was reborn into a life that found meaning in service, love, and seeing others not as obstacles or comparisons, but as souls deeply loved by God.

In response to that newfound meaning, I got involved. I began volunteering in the children's ministry at church. Every weekend, I looked forward to walking into a room full of kids whose laughter and energy reminded me of the unfiltered beauty of creation. Their innocence was refreshing, their questions were raw, and their need for love was simple but profound. It was a gift to sit on the floor with them, tell stories about Jesus in ways they could understand, and be part of shaping the way they saw God.

Sometimes the children would hug me without warning, as if they could feel the love flowing through me wasn't just mine, but something bigger. At other times, their wide-eyed wonder as they asked questions about heaven or forgiveness reminded me of how much adults overcomplicate what is actually pure and simple: that God is love. Those kids became little mirrors, reflecting back to me the joy, curiosity, and honesty I had long buried under layers of self-protection.

I also poured myself into the high school ministry. I was given the chance to sit with a group of ten to twelve young women, week after week, to speak openly about life, choices, faith, and heartbreak. With them, I shared my story in truth, not dressed up or sanitized, but real. I told them what had happened when I led myself astray, when I chose paths that only broke me down. I also told them what redemption looked like. I told them that I lived free from shame, not because I was perfect, but because God's love had covered my imperfections. My hope was that by being honest about my mistakes, I could spare them from repeating some of the same wounds I had carried.

The most beautiful part of those conversations was that the students leaned in. Teenagers have a radar for inauthenticity - they know when you're pretending. When I spoke to them, I saw in their eyes that they were listening, not because I was anyone special, but because I was willing to be real. In being real, they could see the God who was making me whole.

During this same season, my personal life took a turn I could not have predicted. I was training to become a foster parent, a dream that had been growing in me as part of this new outward-focused life. Before that process could fully unfold, my grandmother was diagnosed with Alzheimer's.

There was no question in my mind what I needed to do. I took her into my home. For the next stretch of months, I became her caregiver.

It was not easy. Alzheimer's is a cruel disease. It strips away memory, personality, and dignity piece by piece. Watching someone you love slip away in fragments is heartbreaking. In those long days and nights, I discovered what it meant to serve with love.

I fed her. I cleaned her. I tended to her bedsores. I prayed over her when she was restless. I sang to her when she could not remember who I was. When the time came, I held her hand as she passed from this world into whatever was next for her.

There were moments I wept quietly in the bathroom so she would not see. There were nights I collapsed into bed so exhausted I could barely breathe. Strangely, there was beauty in it too. Alzheimer's stripped away her ability to recognize me, but it also stripped away my need for recognition. I learned to love her without needing her to remember me, to care for her without receiving gratitude, to serve with no expectation of return. That, I realized, was the kind of love God had been trying to teach me all along.

It was one of the most painful and sacred experiences of my life. In caring for her, I learned something new about God's love. It is not glamorous, it is not about recognition, and it is not always easy.

Sometimes it looks like bending low, washing wounds, and offering presence even when words fail. In those quiet moments, I sensed God's nearness more deeply than almost anywhere else.

One thing I quickly realized in this faith-driven life was that walking with God does not exempt me from hardship. Some people imagine that once you "find God," everything suddenly becomes easy, tidy, or perfect. That is not my story.

I still faced questions. I still felt vulnerable at times. Life still delivered pain, uncertainty, and challenges. The difference is this: I no longer faced those things alone.

Instead of being crushed by hardship, I now had a place to bring it. I had a partnership with something far greater than myself, a Creator who could hold my hurts, my confusions, my fears, and my anger without being shaken. With God, I found clarity in the middle of chaos. I found strength in my weakness. While I still had moments that bent me low, they no longer destroyed me. I no longer fell to my knees in despair, but in surrender - that is a very different posture.

This season also brought me face-to-face with questions people have asked for centuries: *If God is real, why is there death? Why is there evil? Why do we suffer?*

Caring for my grandmother forced me to confront death in a very intimate way. What I came to believe was this: death, as painful as it is, can also be a gift.

We are meant to live with the knowledge that our days are numbered, but without knowing exactly how many days we have. That tension is not cruelty. It is mercy. If we lived as though we had forever, we would not value the sacredness of time. We would not feel the urgency to love, forgive, serve, and create.

The gift of death is that it reminds us to live fully. Every single day is an invitation to pour out love, to honor one another, to serve, and to leave a mark that makes the world brighter for the people around us. Knowing that our time is limited frees us from wasting it.

What about evil? That was another question I wrestled with. If God loves us, why does He allow evil to exist?

The answer that grew in my heart was this: because of love.

The greatest gift God has given humanity is free will. He does not force us to love Him, acknowledge Him, or follow Him. Love that is forced is not love at all. It is control. God allows us to choose, and with that freedom comes the reality that people will make choices that cause harm, devastation, and darkness.

Evil exists not because God is absent, but because He is present enough to let us be free. Without the contrast of evil, we would not understand the depth of good. Without experiencing hate, we could not recognize the fullness of love. Though it breaks my heart that some people choose darkness, I can also see the way that God redeems even those moments, using them to strengthen, awaken, and remind us of what is truly worth living for.

Perhaps the most beautiful part of this truth is that God's love does not disappear even when we choose wrongly. He waits. He redeems. He restores. That is what makes His love different from any human love I had ever known. It is patient, unending, and never withdrawn.

That year became the foundation of everything that followed. It was the year I learned to walk in step with my Creator, to see my life not as my own but as part of a greater story. It was the year I discovered that the beauty of life is not in the absence of pain, but in the presence of God through it all.

I was living proof that someone could go from anxiety, self-obsession, and brokenness to peace, purpose, and service. And it was not because I had unlocked some secret within myself. It was not because I had mastered self-help techniques or perfected my habits. It was because I had encountered Love Himself, and that encounter had changed me forever.

Chapter 11

Evolving Grace

One of the most profound ways my life shifted after my encounter with God was in how I began to see the world, people, and myself within the story of humanity. Before that moment, I had lived a life where I often looked at others through the lens of what was missing - what they were not doing right, where they fell short, or how they could be better. I judged, often quietly. Sometimes it was hidden beneath a smile or tucked away under my attempts at kindness, but it was there. I saw people through the broken filter of my own pain, and because I had not fully received grace for my own life, I had very little to extend to anyone else.

Everything changed after God made Himself undeniably real to me. It was as though someone had wiped the fog from the glass I had been peering through for decades. Suddenly, people looked different to me, not because they had changed, but because my heart had. Where once I had been quick to criticize, I now found myself softened. Where once I had measured others by their performance, I now felt called to see them as God's creation, flawed, yes, but beautiful in their struggle, valuable in their humanity, and worthy of love because He had already declared them worthy.

I began to notice small things. The way a cashier's tired eyes carried a story she was not saying out loud. The way a friend's defensiveness was less about me and more about a wound they had not healed. The way strangers carried invisible burdens in their posture, in the way they avoided eye contact, in the way their voices cracked when they tried to sound strong. Before, I would have missed these details or worse, misinterpreted them as weakness or irritation. With new eyes, I saw people as travelers on the same rough road I had been stumbling along for years. I saw them as souls navigating their own storms, longing for belonging, just as I had.

This shift was not instant perfection. It was a daily rewiring of how I thought. Old habits of criticism and impatience still crept in, but I caught them faster. I began pausing in moments where I once would have reacted harshly. When someone cut me off in traffic, instead of cursing under my breath, I found myself thinking, *maybe they are rushing to the hospital. Maybe their heart is racing with fear.* I do not know their story, but God does. When a friend disappointed me, instead of retreating into resentment, I remembered how many times I had disappointed others and how grace had met me in those places. That awareness transformed not only my relationships but also the way I carried myself in the world.

I realized that the same grace God had poured over my life, the grace that pulled me out of brokenness and met me when I was stubborn, self-reliant, and resistant, was the grace He was extending to everyone else. If I had been given that gift so freely, who was I to withhold it from others?

The change also revealed how deeply ingrained judgment had been in me. I had not considered myself a judgmental person, but the truth was that my independence had often made me self-righteous. If I could discipline myself, achieve, and push through pain, then why could others not do the same? I measured worth by effort, and I extended compassion only when I thought it was earned. God shattered that system. He reminded me that love is not earned - it is given. People are not valuable because of their accomplishments. They are valuable because they were created. Worth is not built. It is inherent.

There was one evening that made this reality vivid. I was sitting in a coffee shop, journaling, when a woman walked in. She was disheveled, her clothes wrinkled, her hair tangled, her eyes darting around nervously. In the past, I might have felt uncomfortable.

I might have avoided looking at her, or worse, made a snap judgment about her choices. This time, something stirred in me. I looked at her and thought, that is someone God loves. That is someone He sees fully, someone He aches for, someone He knows by name. My heart softened, and before I knew it, I was smiling at her in a way that felt unforced and genuine. She caught my eye, hesitated, and then smiled back. It was small, but it felt like holy ground, like a reminder that even the smallest gestures of recognition can carry divine weight.

As this transformation deepened, I began to examine not just how I saw strangers, but how I saw the people closest to me, my family, my friends, my coworkers. It is easy to extend grace to someone you do not know, because you are not entangled in their daily choices. Extending grace to the people who hurt you, frustrate you, or continually let you down is where the real work happens.

I thought of my father, of the pain and distance that had lingered between us for years. For so long, I had carried resentment, even if I did not always acknowledge it. I judged him for not being the father I thought I needed. I critiqued his absence, his words, his choices. After my encounter with God, I began to see him differently. He was not just my father who failed me. He was a man with his own wounds, his own history, and his own brokenness that shaped the way he showed up in the world. That did not erase the hurt, but it reframed it. I began to pray for him not out of obligation but out of compassion. I began to ask God to show me how to love him, not for who I wished he was, but for who he truly was, a flawed and beloved child of God.

The same was true for friendships. There were people in my life who drained me, who spoke carelessly, who sometimes betrayed my trust. Before, I would have built walls or cut ties completely. Now I asked different questions. *How can I love them while protecting my own heart? How can I see them the way God does, even if I must step back from closeness?* I realized that grace does not mean permitting harm. It means holding both truth and love in the same hand. It means forgiving while setting boundaries. It means choosing compassion without abandoning wisdom.

This season was also marked by a heightened awareness of the struggles people carried silently. Addiction, depression, financial stress, broken marriages, and strained parent-child relationships. These were not abstract issues anymore. They were living realities in the lives of people sitting across from me at dinner tables, in church pews, and in grocery store lines. Every time I noticed, I felt God's nudge. See them. Really see them. Do not just glance past their pain. Bear witness. Offer kindness. Pray for them, even if silently.

The irony was that in seeing others more clearly, I began to see myself more honestly too. I could no longer cling to the illusion that I was somehow above certain struggles. God reminded me gently, again and again, that the same grace I extended outward had to be received inward. I had to learn to love myself not for my accomplishments or improvements, but simply because I too was His creation. That realization dismantled years of striving and self-criticism.

The beauty of this shift is that it began to ripple outward. My conversations changed. My tone softened. I listened more. I interrupted less. I became more curious about people's stories, more willing to hear perspectives I disagreed with, and more open to learning instead of defending. Grace became not just a theological concept, but a daily practice woven into how I moved through the world.

It was not always easy. There were days when my old self flared up, when judgment came rushing back like an uninvited guest. There were moments when impatience snapped at the heels of compassion, when I caught myself rolling my eyes or speaking harshly. The difference now was that I noticed. I repented quickly. I asked God to realign my heart, to cleanse my vision again, to help me see through His eyes instead of my own. It became a rhythm of falling and rising, of failing and being restored, of learning to love not because it was natural, but because it was divine.

I often think about what the world might look like if we all truly lived this way, if we all saw one another not through the lens of competition, fear, or judgment, but through the lens of grace. How many arguments would dissolve. How many marriages would heal. How many friendships would thrive. How many people would feel less alone. The vision is overwhelming and simple. Love as we have been loved. Forgive as we have been forgiven. See as we have been seen.

This chapter of my life taught me that transformation is not about arriving at perfection. It is about learning a new way of seeing, day by day, moment by moment. It is about choosing, again and again, to see people as God's creation, to remember that we are all stumbling, learning, and longing together. It is about practicing grace in the small moments until it becomes the natural rhythm of your heart.

In the end, what changed most was not the people around me. It was me. My encounter with God gave me eyes to see beauty where I once saw brokenness, a heart to love where I once critiqued, and a patience to walk alongside others as fellow travelers instead of competitors. That is one of the greatest gifts of awakening, to be so transformed by grace that you cannot help but extend it outward.

Chapter 12

The Masks We Wear

Life has a way of teaching us how to perform, and for some of us, those lessons come far too early. I was still just a child when I first learned how to put on a mask, how to smile, nod, and pretend that everything was fine even when my insides were screaming. That mask became my survival tool. It kept people from asking too many questions, shielded the world from seeing the cracks in me, and gave me just enough camouflage to keep going when I didn't have the energy or the safety to explain what was really happening inside. At the time, I believed it was protecting me. I would later learn that masks are heavy, and they slowly suffocate you even as you convince yourself you need them to survive.

I can still remember the first time I consciously put one on. I was young, and something painful had happened, one of those moments where a child should have been comforted, protected, and reassured, but instead, the pain was brushed off or ignored. I realized at that moment that showing pain wasn't safe. If I wanted to make it through, I had to hide it. I smiled. I acted like nothing was wrong. I tucked my truth behind my teeth and convinced the world that I was fine. That was the day I learned how to perform.

From then on, it became second nature. Smile, laugh, perform. Be the strong one. Hold it together. Do not let anyone see the real mess. By the time I reached high school, I was a professional at wearing it. As a teenage mom, I felt the eyes of everyone around me - my peers, teachers, and even strangers - staring, judging, whispering. I wore a mask of confidence that declared, "I can do this," even when I was terrified. I wanted people to believe I was strong because the alternative felt too vulnerable. If they saw how broken and afraid I was inside, if they knew how insecurity consumed me, I was convinced they would use it against me. I held my head high, plastered on that mask, and kept walking.

The irony is that people bought it. They praised me for being so responsible, strong, and put together. They had no idea that behind closed doors, I was crying in bathrooms, lying awake at night consumed by panic, and breaking apart piece by piece. The mask fooled them, but it never healed me. In a world that rewards performance, the mask always got applause. People liked the image I projected because it kept things simple for them. If I smiled, they did not have to ask questions. If I laughed, they did not have to sit with my pain. If I said, "I'm fine," they could nod, move on, and never be inconvenienced.

I kept wearing it, because the world seemed to want the mask more than it wanted me. Every time I heard someone say, "You're so strong, I don't know how you do it," I felt the knife twist a little deeper inside. Because the truth was the opposite. I was not strong. I was not holding it all together. I was barely surviving, and put together was nothing more than tape and glue that could have come apart at any moment.

The problem with masks is that you can only wear them for so long before they start to suffocate you. Pretending is exhausting. It drains your energy to hold up an image that does not match reality. It drains you to choke back tears when you want to collapse, to keep laughing when your heart is breaking. My body began to pay the price for all the pretending. My chest would tighten, my stomach would knot, my shoulders felt like boulders pressing against me. I did not know it then, but later I would understand that trauma does not just live in the mind. It takes up residence in the body. My mask was literally making me sick.

Relationally, I paid an even steeper cost. Wearing a mask means nobody truly knows you. You can be surrounded by people who say they love you, but if they only know the version of you that is performing, that love never penetrates. It feels hollow. It leaves you lonelier than if you were actually alone. There was a day when I looked in the mirror and did not even recognize myself anymore. My eyes looked dull, lifeless. The smile on my face seemed foreign, as if it belonged to a photograph of someone else pasted over my reflection. That was the day I realized I had lost myself underneath all the layers of performance. The mask had become my identity, and I was terrified because I no longer knew who I really was.

What I have come to understand is that almost all of us wear masks at some point in our lives. Some of us wear the "I'm fine" mask that hides heartbreak. Others wear the "successful" mask that conceals insecurity. There are masks that present happy relationships while hiding abuse or disconnection, masks of being a faithful believer while secretly wrestling with doubts, and masks of being the perfect parent while carrying a quiet fear of failing. We put them on for survival, for acceptance, for protection. We put them on because we are afraid, afraid of rejection, afraid of abandonment, afraid that honesty will be punished.

The truth is, though masks may shield us from judgment, they also rob us of intimacy. You cannot be loved for who you really are if no one ever gets to see who you really are. While masks may protect, they also imprison.

Taking mine off did not happen in one dramatic moment. It was a slow, painful process that required courage I was not sure I had. It started with God, because with Him, there was never any mask. He saw me, the me I was trying so desperately to hide from the world. I did not need to perform in prayer, did not need to act strong, did not need to put on my "I'm okay" face. With Him, I could unravel and still be loved. That truth became the foundation for learning how to let my guard down with people too.

It started with small cracks. I remember the first time I admitted to someone I trusted that I was not okay. I let myself cry in front of them instead of running away to cry in private. I spoke honestly about the pain I had buried deep inside. Each time I did, I braced myself for rejection, for judgment, for someone to tell me I was too much or not enough, but that never happened. Instead, I felt lighter. The mask slipped, and the world did not end.

Over time, I realized I did not have to perform anymore. I could be free. Free to cry without apology. Free to laugh when it was genuine instead of when it was expected. Free to say, "I'm struggling," without drowning in shame. That freedom began to change everything. My relationships became deeper because people were finally able to connect with the real me. My body began to heal as it no longer had to carry the constant tension of pretending. My faith deepened because I stopped trying to perform for God and started resting in the truth that He already knew every part of me and loved me still. Most importantly of all, I began to recognize myself again.

Stepping out from behind the mask also forced me to confront how often I had chosen relationships with people who only wanted the performance, not the person. That realization was painful. I had to accept that some of the love I thought I had was not really mine. It belonged to the version of me I had constructed. And when that version was gone, so was their affection. At first, losing those people felt like rejection, but eventually I came to see it as protection. God was pruning away what could not sustain me so that I could grow into who I truly was meant to be.

I also learned that vulnerability attracts vulnerability. The moment I began letting others see my real self, people around me started to open up too. I was stunned at how many people were also hiding, pretending, and suffocating beneath the weight of their own masks. When I dared to go first and admitted my cracks, it gave them permission to take their own masks off. Some of the deepest, most authentic relationships of my life were born this way, not in perfection, but in shared honesty.

There were still moments when I reached for the mask out of habit. Old patterns die hard, and fear does not disappear overnight. Every time I picked it back up, I felt its weight immediately. It was no longer comfortable, no longer bearable. I had tasted freedom, and once you have breathed that air, pretending feels unbearable. Slowly, I learned to choose authenticity again and again, until it became my new way of life.

I know what it feels like to be exhausted from pretending. I know how it feels to want so badly to be seen but to be terrified of what will happen if you are truly honest. I can tell you this. You do not have to keep wearing the mask. It may have protected you once, but it is not serving you anymore. It is keeping you from the love, connection, and healing you were created for.

Taking it off will not feel easy. It feels like standing naked in the storm, exposed and trembling. But the freedom that waits on the other side is worth it. Because here is the truth: the people who are meant to love you will love you even more when they see the real you, and the people who cannot handle the truth of who you are were never truly loving you in the first place. They were only ever loving the mask. Losing them is not a loss. It is a release.

The masks we wear may help us survive, but they can never help us truly live. At some point, each of us has to decide if survival is enough, or if we want freedom. For me, survival kept me alive, but freedom finally allowed me to breathe. And choosing freedom, choosing to be fully myself without apology, has been one of the bravest, hardest, and most beautiful choices I have ever made.

And still, there were quieter lessons the mask taught me as it loosened. I began to notice how often I used humor to redirect hard conversations, how often I asked others questions so I would not have to answer my own. I noticed the way my voice lifted half a note when I said, "I'm good," as if I could sing my way into being okay. These little tells became invitations to pause. I would feel the urge to perform and choose a breath instead. I would hear the script begin to play and choose a truer sentence. The first attempts were choppy and awkward. The more I practiced, the more natural honesty became.

There was a night in the kitchen with my son when the mask slipped and did not return. He asked me if I was okay. I said yes out of habit, then stopped and tried again. I told him I was tired and a little scared about something I could not control, but I was working through it. His shoulders softened. He did not need me to be perfect. He needed me to be real. That simple exchange rewired something in me. Masks demand distance. Honesty creates room to breathe.

I also learned that taking off the mask is not the same as spilling everything. There is a sacred difference between secrecy and privacy. Secrecy hides truth because it fears judgment. Privacy guards the truth because it honors timing and trust. I began to practice sharing the right truths with the right people at the right time. That practice kept me safe without sending me back into hiding. It allowed me to be open without being exposed.

As the mask fell away, my body responded. Sleep returned in longer stretches. My jaw was unclenched. The knot that lived under my ribs softened. I started to recognize how often my body had sounded the alarm while my words insisted I was fine. Learning to listen to my body became part of learning to live unmasked. A tight chest meant I needed a walk. A sore throat meant I had swallowed too many unsaid sentences. A pounding head meant I had nodded yes when I meant no. My body became a compass pointing toward truth.

Not everyone celebrated the change. Some people preferred the version of me who never asked for anything, who never disagreed, who wore composure like a uniform. When I began to say no without long explanations, a few pulled back. I let them. The room got quieter, but it also got clearer. The friends who stayed sat closer. They asked better questions. They told harder truths with gentleness. We learned to meet one another without costumes. The love in that space felt weighty and clean.

Freedom did not make me fearless. It made me faithful. I still felt the flutter of anxiety when I told the truth. I still had moments when I wanted to make everything neat with a quick joke or a polished answer. The difference is that I kept choosing honesty anyway. Courage was not a roaring feeling. Courage was four words said plainly. I am not OK. Courage was another four. I need help. Courage was the smallest sentence I learned to love. No.

If I could gather every mask I ever wore, I imagine they would fill a room. The polished one for work. The unbreakable one for family. The agreeable one for friends. I do not hate those masks. They kept me alive when I did not have better tools. I simply refuse to live behind them now. They are part of my past, not my present. I bless them for their service, and I leave them on the shelf.

Choosing authenticity did not make life easier, but it made life honest, where real connection can grow. Honest life is where grief can be held and joy can be felt without apology. Honest life is where God meets me, not at the edge of performance, but in the middle of my unvarnished truth.

This is how I live now. Not flawlessly. Not loudly. Simply, steadily, without the mask. The air is finally good to breathe.

Chapter 13

Healing Generational Wounds

When I look back at the course of my life, one of the most striking realizations is how much of who we become is shaped not only by our choices, but also by the choices of those who came before us. We inherit more than eye color or family traditions. We inherit patterns - some beautiful, some destructive. If we are not intentional, those patterns repeat themselves across generations like a song stuck on replay, echoing through families without anyone ever questioning where the music began.

I didn't fully grasp this until years into my journey of faith and healing. For most of my life, I assumed that the dysfunction I witnessed or the struggles I carried were simply who I was. I didn't recognize how many of those behaviors, fears, and coping mechanisms were passed down to me, handed from one set of wounded hands to another, like heirlooms nobody wanted but everyone carried. When you're a child, you don't question it - you take the environment around you as truth.

At some point, if you are brave enough, you stop and ask, *Does this really have to continue?*

The truth is, every family has cycles. Some of them are life giving: resilience, generosity, a strong work ethic, creativity, and loyalty. Others are toxic: addiction, anger, silence, codependency, abuse, and secrets. Until someone names them, they weave themselves invisibly into the fabric of our lives, convincing us that this is just the way it is.

I remember the first time I really saw the cycle in my own family. It was like someone had turned on the lights in a dark room. Suddenly, I saw the thread of brokenness weaving its way through stories of relatives and generations I had barely thought about before. I saw the unspoken patterns of pain, ways of coping, ways of avoiding, ways of controlling, that felt eerily familiar to me because I was living them too.

That realization both crushed me and freed me. It crushed me because it meant that my struggles were not random, they were inherited. It freed me because it meant I was not powerless. Cycles can be broken. Legacies can be rewritten. Pain can be stopped from traveling forward if someone is willing to stand in the gap and say, "This ends with me."

The hardest part of breaking generational cycles is that so many of them are invisible until you step back far enough to see them. For years, I thought my anxiety was simply my problem. I thought my drive to please people and avoid conflict was part of my personality. I thought my tendency to push myself to exhaustion was ambition. It took me a long time to realize those were survival mechanisms that had been modeled for me long before I even knew their names.

Children absorb the unspoken. They watch how parents handle stress, how they argue, how they love, how they grieve. They notice what is allowed to be said out loud and what must be buried in silence. They learn what earns approval and what draws shame. Before they even realize it, those lessons shape who they become.

In my family, silence was often the mask. Hard things were not discussed. Pain was brushed under the rug. You smiled, you kept going, you pretended. That silence taught me that my feelings were inconvenient, that honesty was dangerous, that pretending was safer. Without even thinking about it, I learned to put on my own mask, the same way those before me had.

It was not just silence, though. There was also fear. A fear of being truly seen, of being rejected, of not measuring up. That fear carried through relationships like a shadow. I carried it too, without ever asking if it really belonged to me.

One of the bravest things a person can do is ask, "Why?"

Why do we keep repeating this?

Why do we keep choosing pain instead of healing?

Why do we allow anger, addiction, shame, or silence to keep leading the story?

Those questions are terrifying because they threaten the foundation – even an unhealthy foundation - that has held the family together, but they are also the key to freedom.

I remember sitting alone one night, journaling, and writing the words, "I do not want my child to inherit this." That was the moment I knew the cycle had to break. I could not undo what had already been passed down to me, but I could stop handing it forward. I could choose differently. I could give the next generation something better.

Here is the truth I have come to believe. When you decide to break a cycle, you are not just fighting for yourself. You are fighting for everyone who comes after you. You are planting a new tree in soil that has been dry for too long. You are writing a new chapter in a story that has been stuck in repetition.

What people do not always tell you is that breaking generational cycles is not glamorous. It is not a single, dramatic moment of change. It is often a daily, exhausting choice. It requires awareness, honesty, and courage. It requires therapy, prayer, and boundaries. It requires saying no to what has always been normal and yes to what feels terrifyingly new.

For me, it looked like admitting truths I had been running from for decades. It looked like sitting in a counselor's office and saying words out loud that had been buried in silence. It looked like telling family members no when they expected me to keep playing the same role I always had. It looked like disappointing people who preferred the mask version of me to the real one.

Breaking cycles often means becoming the black sheep of the family, the one who disrupts the unspoken rules, the one who refuses to keep pretending. It can feel lonely. It can make you question yourself. It can also be the most sacred work you ever do.

As much as it costs, the alternative costs more. Continuing the cycle means watching the people you love suffer in the same ways you have. It means passing down the same wounds to children and grandchildren, choosing comfort over transformation. I could not live with that.

For me, faith became the anchor in this process. Left to my own strength, I would have collapsed under the weight of it. The pull of old patterns is strong. The temptation to return to what is familiar, even if it is destructive, is constant. However, God gave me a new framework, a new way of being.

In Scripture, I found reminders that I was not defined by what came before me. I was not doomed to repeat the mistakes of generations past. I was a new creation, invited into freedom rather than bondage. "Therefore, if anyone is in Christ, he is a new creation; the old has gone, the new has come" (2 Corinthians 5:17). I learned that God's desire was not punishment, but restoration, not shame, but renewal. "The Lord is close to the brokenhearted and saves those who are crushed in spirit" (Psalm 34:18). I began to understand that while patterns may be inherited, they are not permanent. Through God's grace, cycles can be interrupted and rewritten. "But where sin increased, grace increased all the more" (Romans 5:20).

That truth became my lifeline. On the days I wanted to give up, I reminded myself that I was not just fighting my own battles. I was standing in the gap for future generations. I was building something new on a foundation that could last.

Faith also helped me learn forgiveness. Part of breaking cycles means learning to see those who came before you with compassion. It is easy to turn blame into bitterness. It is harder to recognize that those who hurt you were often just repeating the patterns they inherited. They were wearing masks of their own, carrying wounds of their own. Forgiveness does not excuse their choices, but it does release you from carrying their burden as your own.

What does it look like to live free from the cycles that once defined you?

For me, it looks like speaking when silence would feel easier. It looks like being honest about my struggles instead of hiding them. It looks like choosing healthy relationships instead of repeating toxic ones. It looks like pausing before reacting, asking myself, "Is this me, or is this the old pattern talking?"

It also looks like creating new rhythms in my family. It means telling the truth even when it is uncomfortable. It means apologizing when I mess up, instead of pretending I am fine. It means modeling vulnerability so that others know it is safe to be real.

It is not about perfection. It is about presence. It is about showing up differently so that the story being written forward is not just a repeat of the one behind.

Here's the thing about cycles. When you break them, you do not just create freedom for yourself. You create space for others to step into freedom too. I have seen it in my friendships, family, and community. When one person is brave enough to tell the truth, it gives others permission to do the same. When one person refuses to keep playing the same role, it opens the door for others to step into new ones.

I sometimes think about the generations that will come after me - children, grandchildren, great grandchildren - and I imagine them standing on a foundation stronger than the one I was handed. I imagine them living free from the fear, silence, and shame. I imagine them carrying forward not the wounds, but the wisdom. That thought alone makes every painful step of this journey worth it.

The truth is, breaking cycles is not a one-time decision. It is a choice you make every single day. Some days it is easier. Some days it feels impossible. Every day is an opportunity to keep building something new.

There are still moments when I feel the pull of old patterns, when I want to put the mask back on, avoid, and react the way I always used to. Then I remember, I am not bound to those cycles anymore. I have a choice. Every time I choose differently, I step further into the freedom that was always waiting for me.

Breaking the cycle does not mean erasing the past. It means transforming it. It means taking the ashes of what was and letting God breathe beauty into them. It means carrying forward not the weight of wounds, but the strength of healing.

With every step forward, I remind myself, I am not just living for me. I am living for every soul who will come after me. I am choosing freedom so they can inherit it. I am breaking the cycle so they do not have to.

That, to me, is the true meaning of legacy. Here's how that legacy began to look in the day to day.

There was a holiday dinner when the old script tried to run itself. Voices tightened over the table, old grievances rising like steam from hot plates. I felt the familiar tug to smooth it all over, to swallow my truth, to keep the peace at any cost. Instead, I put my fork down and said, calmly and without apology, "I love you, and I am not willing to continue this conversation in a way that hurts us. I am stepping outside to breathe, and I will come back when we are ready to speak kindly." No one clapped and no one thanked me, but the air shifted. A new line had been drawn, not as punishment, but as protection. That is what boundary work looked like in real time, quiet and steady.

There was a morning when I sat at the kitchen table with a pen and a sheet of paper and drew a simple family map. Names, arrows, and little notes in the margins: what was said, what was not said, who drank, who raged, who went silent, who carried, who performed. Seeing it on paper took the shame out of my chest and set it down where I could touch it. The pattern was no longer a fog. It had edges. When something has edges, you can begin to reshape it.

There was an afternoon in a counselor's office when I practiced saying the words I had never heard in my house growing up. "I am sorry." "I was wrong." "Please forgive me." "Thank you for telling me the truth." The first time I said them out loud, they felt awkward in my mouth, like a language I had not learned to speak. However, repetition softens fear. These phrases became tools I carried home and used with the people I love. They were small keys, and small keys open real doors.

There was a night I sat on the edge of my son's bed and told him, with a steady voice and an open heart, that I was learning to do things differently. I named the ways I had protected peace at the expense of truth. I named the places I had confused performance with love. I told him he was free to tell me when I repeated old patterns, and that I would listen. He nodded slowly, taking in my words the way a field takes in rain. That was a moment when the future shifted an inch.

There was a decision to leave a conversation unfinished rather than finish it in anger. There was a choice to rest instead of proving worth through exhaustion. There was a practice of sending a text to a friend that said, "I am tempted to disappear. Please check on me tomorrow." Each small decision was a thread. Over time, threads become fabric. Over time, fabric becomes shelter.

There were prayers that did not sound pretty. "God, I want to go back to what I know. Help me not to." "God, I want to say yes to make them happy. Help me say the honest no." "God, I want to carry what is not mine. Help me set it down." These prayers did not make me perfect. They made me present. They taught me to pause long enough to let wisdom arrive.

There was forgiveness that came like a tide, slow and faithful. Not a feeling that erased the past, but a posture that refused to keep drinking the poison. I wrote letters I never sent. I imagined handing back what was not mine to carry. I pictured myself at the foot of a cross, emptying pockets full of other people's fears. I walked away lighter, not because the past had changed, but because the hold it had on me had loosened.

There was a new kind of celebration. Not the loud party where we pretend the bruises are not there, but the quiet meal where we bless what is true. We named the win when someone told the hard truth. We named the miracle when someone took a breath rather than raise a voice. We blessed small steps the way you bless seedlings, tender and worth protecting.

There was a blessing I began to speak over my house: "May the truth feel safe here. May rest be honored here. May apology be quick here. May love outlast fear here." I whispered it while I washed dishes. I spoke it while I folded towels. I wrote it on a card and taped it inside the pantry door where only I would see it. It changed me first, then it changed the room.

This is the real work of breaking cycles. Not the dramatic scene, but the everyday practice. Not the perfect apology, but the honest one. Not the instant transformation, but the faithful turn in a new direction again and again.

I still have days when the old music tries to pull me back onto the familiar dance floor. I still feel the itch to perform, the urge to pacify, the rush to over function when silence stretches between people I love. On those days, I remember that legacy is built in inches. I remember that new roots take time. I remember that I am not doing this alone.

I keep choosing. I choose the pause. I choose the truth. I choose the boundary that makes love possible. I choose to bless what is growing rather than curse what is not yet finished. With every choice, I hear the old song grow a little quieter while a new one, steady and clear, takes its place.

That is how generational wounds become generational wisdom. That is how the story changes.

That is how a life, and then a family, and then a future, is healed.

Chapter 14

Planting New Roots

When I look back on the arc of my life, it sometimes feels as though there are two stories unfolding at once. There is the story of what was handed to me - patterns, pain, habits, expectations, cycles that felt unshakable - and the story of what I chose to do with it all. For years, it seemed like I had no choice, as though the ground beneath me had already been tilled and seeded by someone else's hands. I was simply expected to live out the harvest, whether it bore fruit or thorns. The truth I have discovered, slowly and sometimes painfully, is that while I may not have been able to choose the soil I was born into, I do get to choose the roots I plant now.

That realization did not come easily. For so long, survival was my focus. I was too busy trying to outrun the weight of my past to consider the future I might be capable of building. However, life has a way of pressing pause, of forcing you to sit in the quiet and take stock.

There came a point when I began to realize that I was no longer simply surviving. I was being asked to live, to build, to plant, and that is a far scarier thing. Surviving demands grit. Living demands courage. Surviving asks you to hold on. Living asks you to let go and begin again.

Planting new roots is not glamorous work. It is slow, patient, and often invisible. When you put a seed in the ground, you do not see the change immediately. Days, weeks, even months can pass before the first sign of life pushes through the soil. In that waiting, you are tempted to wonder if anything is happening at all. Beneath the surface, where no one can see, roots are reaching, strengthening, and anchoring themselves to something solid. That is how I feel about the work I began in this next chapter of my life, the quiet, unseen work of creating something new.

The hardest part was believing I was even capable of it. For years, the voices in my head had convinced me otherwise. They told me I would always repeat the same mistakes, that I would never break free from what was handed to me. They told me hope was naïve, that dreaming of something better was setting myself up for disappointment. There was another whisper, softer but steadier, that said: *What if you could? What if this time could be different? What if there is more for you?*

Hope is a fragile thing at first. It is like holding a tiny flame cupped in your hands while the wind threatens to snuff it out. You guard it, protect it, and wonder if it will survive. If you nurture it, hope grows stronger. It takes root. Eventually, it becomes a fire that no storm can extinguish.

In the beginning, my new roots did not look like much. They looked like small decisions, choosing honesty when silence felt safer, choosing rest when exhaustion tried to prove my worth, choosing boundaries when guilt told me to keep giving myself away. Each choice felt insignificant in the moment, but together they became the foundation of a new way of living. That is the thing about planting. It rarely feels dramatic in the moment, but over time it grows into something unrecognizable from what came before.

I also began to notice how planting new roots changed the way I saw relationships. For so long, I had surrounded myself with people who mirrored the cycles I was trying to escape. I did not realize it at the time, but I was choosing what felt familiar, even when familiar was toxic. Planting something new meant being intentional about who I let into my soil. It meant asking: Does this person water me or drain me? Do they cultivate growth or stifle it? Do they know the real me, or only the mask I used to wear?

It was not an easy process. In fact, it often felt like pruning, a painful cutting away of what no longer served me. Some relationships ended. Some shifted into new shapes. Some revealed truths I did not want to see. But pruning, though it hurts, is necessary for growth. A tree cannot thrive if it keeps feeding dead branches. And neither can a soul.

At the same time, I was learning to celebrate the beauty of new growth, even in its smallest forms. A conversation where I was honest instead of pretending. A night's sleep without the weight of panic pressing on my chest. A moment where laughter felt genuine, not forced. These moments were not dramatic, but they were real. And for the first time in a long time, they felt like me.

Faith, for me, was not a loud declaration during this season. It was more like a steady undercurrent. It was the quiet trust that the soil I was planting in was good, even when I could not see the results yet. It was believing that every act of honesty, every healthy boundary, every new choice mattered, even when it felt small. It was trusting that God, in His own timing, would breathe life into what I was nurturing. I did not always feel strong in that faith, but even the smallest seed of it was enough to keep me going.

What I have learned is that planting new roots is not just about what you let go of. It is about what you choose to carry forward. From the past, I carried resilience. I carried empathy. I carried the wisdom that comes only from walking through fire and surviving it.

Those became the nutrients in the soil of my new life. Because planting does not mean denying the past. It means transforming it. The ashes of what was can still feed the ground for what is to come.

One of the greatest joys of this season has been watching how my choices ripple outward. Just as cycles of pain can echo through generations, so can cycles of healing. I see it in my child when he chooses to speak truth instead of hiding. I see it in my friendships when vulnerability becomes an invitation for deeper connection. I see it in myself when I recognize I am no longer defined by fear, but by freedom. These ripples remind me that the work of planting is never just for yourself. It is always for others, too.

Here's is the part that continues to amaze me. Life does not just ask us to plant once - it asks us to keep planting, again and again. Each new season requires new roots, new courage, and new beginnings. Some of what I planted has already grown strong and steady. Some of it is still fragile, still reaching. Some of it will take years before I see the fruit, but that is the nature of planting. You trust the process, even when you cannot see the outcome yet.

There are still days when I feel the temptation to return to old soil. Days when fear whispers that it would be easier to slip back into familiar patterns. Days when loneliness tempts me to settle for relationships that do not honor the roots I am nurturing. Then I remember the quiet strength of the seeds I have already planted. I remember the weight of what I have already survived, and I remind myself: I am building something new.

Hope, I have realized, is not a destination. It is a practice. Every day I choose it, even when it feels small, even when it feels hard. Every day I remind myself that the story I am writing now is not the story I was handed. Every day I believe, even just a little more, that freedom is not only possible, it is mine.

Planting new roots has taught me patience, perseverance, and presence. It has taught me to honor the slow work of transformation. It has shown me that beginnings do not always look like fireworks. Sometimes they look like a seed in the dark, quietly stretching toward the light.

Maybe that is the most important lesson of all. Growth is rarely loud. It is quiet, steady, and faithful. It is choosing to believe in what you cannot yet see. It is trusting that even in the dark, life is happening.

I keep planting. I keep tending. I keep believing that the roots I nurture now will grow into a legacy of freedom, hope, and love. Not just for me, but for everyone who comes after me. Because in the end, planting new roots is not only about creating a life you can stand in. It is about leaving behind soil where others can flourish, too.

There is another truth I have learned. Planting requires surrender. You do not control the rain, the sun, or the seasons. You can water, nurture, and protect, but ultimately, growth has a timing of its own. I used to fight against that, wanting instant results and proof that all my effort was worth it. Now I see that the waiting is its own sacred teacher. Waiting teaches humility. Waiting teaches trust. Waiting reminds me that life is not meant to be rushed - it is meant to be lived.

There are moments when I walk outside and see a tree, tall and steady, and I think about how it once was nothing more than a fragile sprout. No one clapped when it broke through the soil. No one noticed its slow growth year after year. Here it stands, rooted, weathered, alive. That is the kind of strength I want my life to hold. Not flashy, not temporary, but steady, the kind of strength that weathers storms because its roots are deep.

Here's the beauty. Planting new roots does not mean erasing the old story. It means redeeming it. It means taking everything I have endured, all the brokenness and survival, and allowing it to become part of the soil where something better can grow. It means honoring where I have been, but refusing to let it dictate where I am going. It means standing in the tension of both grief and gratitude. Grief for what I lost. Gratitude for what I have gained.

When I think about legacy now, I do not picture wealth or accomplishments or accolades. I picture soil. I picture deep, rich ground that is safe for others to plant in. I picture future generations standing stronger because I chose to dig deep and plant something different. That is the inheritance I want to leave behind. Not just stories of survival, but living proof of transformation.

Because at the end of it all, planting new roots is an act of defiance. It is looking at the patterns that tried to destroy you and saying, "You do not win." It is choosing to write a new story when the old one seemed certain. It is standing in the ashes of what was and daring to believe that beauty can still grow here.

I believe it can.

Chapter 15

Choosing Joy, Contentment, and Peace

When I look at my life today, there are times I hardly recognize it. If someone had told me ten years ago that I would be living on a ranch in a small city I never imagined calling home, surrounded by more than sixteen animals, caring for my aging parents, and finding fulfillment not in chasing the next achievement but in serving others, I might have laughed in disbelief. Back then, joy meant something very different to me. Joy looked like accomplishments, recognition, validation, and the illusion of control. It looked like more, more success, more love, more possessions, more approval. But today, joy has taken on a quieter, deeper, and more enduring shape. It looks like feeding my animals in the early morning light, hearing their hooves and paws move across the earth. It looks like holding my parents' hands as they grow older, offering back the care they once gave to me. It looks like choosing service over ego, presence over performance, and peace over striving.

There was a time when I would have rolled my eyes at that description of joy. I would have thought it sounded too plain, too small, too ordinary to be worth aspiring to. The truth is, the kind of joy that sustains a soul rarely comes dressed in glamour. It is born in the quiet rhythms we learn to cherish when the noise fades, the applause stops, and the only thing left is the life you actually live. I didn't know it then, but joy was waiting for me in the very spaces I once dismissed as insignificant.

The truth is, I am only here because of everything that came before. Every wound, every heartbreak, every battle, every season of waiting has been the soil that brought me to this place. I did not design this life. Left to my own plans, I would have drawn up something entirely different. I would have chosen glamour over grit, comfort over challenge, applause over humility. God had a better story, even if it took years of breaking and rebuilding for me to see it. Standing here, I realize joy is not about getting everything we thought we wanted, but is about discovering that what God gives us is far richer than what we could have imagined for ourselves.

That realization didn't come all at once. It was layered, like the slow growth of a tree whose rings can only be counted with time. In some seasons I fought against it, stubbornly holding to the belief that I knew better, that my picture of happiness was the right one. Each loss, disappointment, and heartbreak stripped away another layer of that illusion. Only then did I begin to see that what I once thought was failure was actually God's gentle redirection. The story He was writing wasn't smaller than mine - it was fuller, richer, and rooted in eternity rather than ego.

For most of my life, I believed joy would come when the circumstances finally aligned, when I reached a goal, when I found the right relationship, when the wounds of my past stopped aching. I treated joy as something that waited for me on the other side of "someday." But the journey of these past chapters has taught me that joy is not a prize at the finish line. Joy is a practice. Joy is a lens. Joy is a choice that reshapes how we see the very same circumstances that once weighed us down.

That shift, from waiting for joy to choosing it, has been one of the most freeing lessons of my life. I used to imagine joy as a locked door, with the key always out of reach. I've come to see joy as a window that has always been open, waiting for me to notice. The air of joy was always there - I just had to stop suffocating myself with the stale air of striving to breathe it in.

It hasn't been easy. Choosing joy, especially in a world that tells us to chase more, has required me to shift my entire perspective. The world insists that success is measured by accumulation, more money, more followers, more recognition, more comfort. That pursuit of "more" is endless, and in chasing it, I found myself emptier than before. My soul was constantly hungry and my heart was constantly restless. It took breaking down, losing what I thought defined me, and walking through valleys of pain to finally understand: joy doesn't come from adding to your life - it comes from noticing what's already here, and from serving, giving, and living in alignment with God's design rather than the world's demands.

I often think about the word contentment. For years, it was foreign to me. I mistook contentment for complacency, as though being content meant settling for less than what you deserved. What I've come to learn is that contentment is not about settling, it is about freedom. It is freedom from the endless treadmill of comparison. Freedom from needing to prove your worth through accomplishments. Freedom from believing that peace lies just beyond the next purchase, the next promotion, the next relationship. Contentment is not giving up on dreams, it is simply anchoring yourself in gratitude for what is, rather than constantly living in what if.

Contentment has not dulled my dreams - it has sharpened them. It has taught me to dream from a place of gratitude rather than scarcity, from trust instead of fear. It allows me to reach for more while being deeply at peace with enough. I've learned that paradox is where real freedom lives. When you are no longer ruled by what you don't have, you are finally free to savor what you do.

Peace, too, has changed for me. Once, I thought peace meant the absence of problems. Now I know that peace is not the absence of storms, but the presence of God within them. Peace is the steady assurance that even when life feels unpredictable, I am held. It is the quiet confidence that I don't need to control everything, because the One who holds the universe also holds me.

Peace, I've found, is a posture more than a feeling. It doesn't always silence the noise around me, but it keeps the noise from controlling me. It is like standing in the eye of the storm, chaos swirling, winds howling, and yet somehow knowing you are safe. That kind of peace is not natural; it is supernatural. It is what allows me to walk through seasons I once thought would break me without losing my footing.

This is not the life I planned, but it is the life I was meant for. If not for everything I endured, the heartbreaks, the losses, the betrayals, the healing, the rebuilding, I would not be here. I would not be caring for my parents in their later years, learning patience and tenderness in the most ordinary, sacred ways. I would not be waking up every morning to the sound of animals depending on me, reminding me that service is not glamorous but deeply grounding. I would not be living in this city, on this soil, with this perspective. Most importantly, I would not know the joy that comes from giving instead of grasping, from pouring out instead of hoarding, from letting go instead of holding on so tightly.

The ranch has taught me lessons that no book ever could. There is something about tending to animals that reminds you of the simplicity of life. They do not care about appearances, status, or reputation. They care about consistency, presence, and care. They remind me that life is not about impressing but about nurturing. They remind me that love is not complicated, it is faithful. In their quiet company, I have found a peace that eluded me in rooms filled with noise and applause.

Sometimes, as I walk across the pastures, I can feel the presence of God in the most ordinary details: the crunch of hay under my boots, the way the horses nuzzle close, the sound of the wind threading through the fence lines. It reminds me that joy is not something I have to chase into faraway places. It is right here, stitched into the everyday fabric of my life, waiting to be noticed.

Caring for my parents has also been a profound gift. It is not always easy - aging brings challenges, and stepping into the role of caretaker requires patience and sacrifice. It is in this role that I see the full circle of love. The ones who once carried me now lean on me. While the world often idolizes independence, I have found joy in dependence, the dependence of family, community, and generations caring for one another. It has shown me that selflessness is not about losing yourself - it is about finding a deeper version of yourself in the act of love.

Joy has become less about moments of elation and more about moments of presence. It is the smile on my father's face when I bring him his coffee. It is the gentle sound of animals settling in the barn at night. It is the quiet evenings when I sit outside, watching the sky change colors, knowing that I am exactly where I am supposed to be. Ten years ago, I would not have defined those moments as joy. I would have dismissed them as ordinary, too small to count. Now, I see them as the very heartbeat of life.

Choosing joy does not mean life is easy. There are still challenges. There are still days when I feel the pull of old patterns, when I want to measure myself by the world's standards, when I want to prove, when I want to strive. But each time I face that temptation, I remember what I have already walked through. I remember that chasing more left me empty. I remember that joy built on ego crumbles, but joy built on service and gratitude endures. Even when it feels unnatural, I choose joy again.

Joy, contentment, and peace are not trophies you win once and keep forever. They are practices. They are seeds you plant daily. Some days, the soil feels hard and the growth feels invisible. Some days, it feels easier to give in to frustration or comparison. Over time, with faith and persistence, those seeds grow roots. They become part of who you are. Before you know it, you realize that what once felt impossible has become your natural way of living.

There are moments when I sit back and think: *I never could have written this story.* That's the beauty of it. When I release my grip on control, when I stop trying to dictate every detail, I leave space for God to do what only He can do. He has given me a life richer than I ever dreamed, not because it is perfect or glamorous, but because it is real, rooted, and purposeful.

The world will always tell us to want more. More recognition, more possessions, more achievement. I've learned that the greatest joy comes not in more, but in enough. It comes in waking up with gratitude. It comes in serving quietly. It comes in knowing that peace and joy are not things the world gives, they are things the world cannot take away.

I choose joy. I choose contentment. I choose peace. In doing so, I find myself living a life I never thought I wanted, but one I would never trade. Because this life, this quiet, rooted, giving, faithful life, is more abundant than anything I could have imagined for myself.

This, to me, is the true definition of joy: not the fleeting thrill of getting what you want, but the enduring gift of discovering that what you have is enough. And in that discovery, you find peace that cannot be shaken, contentment that cannot be stolen, and joy that cannot be silenced.

And maybe the greatest surprise of all is that joy is not just an emotion, it is a legacy. When we choose joy, when we model contentment, when we carry peace, it plants seeds in the lives of everyone who witnesses it. My child sees it, my friends feel it, strangers sense it in the way I carry myself. Joy multiplies. Peace spreads. Contentment invites others to rest. And in that ripple effect, joy becomes not just the story of my life, but a gift that outlives me.

Chapter 16

Reframing Love

For so long, I thought love had to look like what I saw in the movies or read in storybooks. I thought it meant finding the one person who would complete me, who would fill all the cracks and silence all the doubts. I thought love was something you achieved when you finally became worthy enough, beautiful enough, successful enough. When that version of love didn't come in the way I expected, I felt cheated, as though life had withheld something from me.

I have come to learn that love is not confined to the narrow definitions we have been taught. Love is not a single story or a single person. Love is a presence, a lens, a way of being in the world. Love is God Himself, woven through everything that breathes. When you begin to see it that way, you realize that you are never without it.

I used to ache for love to come and rescue me, to prove that I was enough. Now I see that love was around me all along, waiting for me to notice it. It was there in the steady faithfulness of God, who never let go of me even when I let go of Him. It was there in the resilience I carried through heartbreak, in the laughter of my child, in the loyalty of true friends who stayed when others left. It was there in the quiet mornings on the ranch, the soft nuzzle of an animal, the way the sky breaks open with color at sunset. Love is not missing from my life. Love is the very fabric of my life.

We live in a culture that tells us love only counts if it looks a certain way, if it is romantic, grand, celebrated. I have learned that love is much bigger than that. Love is found in the way you forgive yourself after failure. Love is in the patience you offer your aging parents as they lean on you in new ways. Love is in the choice to show up when no one is watching, to give when there is nothing in it for you, to believe the best when life tempts you toward cynicism.

Love is not reserved for the mountaintop moments. It is not just for weddings, anniversaries, or storybook romances. Love shows up in the most ordinary places, if only we are willing to notice it. It can be found in the quiet rhythm of rain against a window, reminding us that life keeps moving, nourishing, and renewing. It is in the way a tree bends with the wind yet still stands rooted, teaching us that strength and flexibility can coexist. It is in the soft nuzzle of an animal who trusts you, or the unfiltered laughter of children discovering joy in the smallest things. These are not small scraps of love - they are evidence that love is woven into the very fabric of our days.

To live awake to love is to recognize it in every breath we take. The moment our feet hit the floor in the morning, we have already received a gift that is bigger than we realize: the gift of another day, another chance to experience this life. Even when hardships come, even when pain or loss meet us in the hours ahead, love is still present in the fact that we are here to feel, to grow, to stumble, to learn. Life itself is a love letter, written in opportunities for us to keep becoming.

Love is also found in the places we least expect. In mistakes that humble us, in forgiveness that frees us, in the messiness of being human. When we choose to forgive ourselves instead of carrying shame, we are choosing love. When we extend grace to others, even when they may not deserve it, we are choosing love. These choices may not feel glamorous, but they are where love does its deepest work.

Love is never more evident than when we give it away. Serving others, whether in our families, our friendships, or our communities, has a way of returning love to us multiplied. Holding the hand of someone who is lonely, sharing a meal with someone in need, listening without judgment - these acts remind us that love is not a scarce resource but an endless flow. The more we give, the more we discover we already have.

What truly shifted everything for me was the epiphany that God's love does not come with conditions. For so much of my life, I had been chasing a version of love that had strings attached. If I was good enough, I could be loved. If I was successful enough, I could be loved. If I was beautiful enough, I could be loved. God showed me that His love is not earned. His love is not dependent on my performance. He loved me in the fullness of who I was, even in the moments when I was broken, making mistakes, sinning, or turning away from Him. He loved me when I was complaining instead of being grateful. He loved me when I thought I had ruined too much to be redeemed. And in realizing that, I discovered the freedom of unconditional love. I no longer had to beg another person to give me what God had already poured out in abundance.

That truth not only reframed my understanding of love but also reframed the way I loved myself. For years I carried shame like a second skin, convinced that my worth was fragile and conditional. Unconditional love shatters shame, reminding you that nothing you do can make God love you more, and nothing you do can make Him love you less. To live out of that truth is to finally exhale. To live out of that truth is to finally believe that you are not just enough, you are beloved.

When I think about love now, I no longer confine it to one story or one definition. Love is in nature, in service, in forgiveness, in presence. Love is in the sunlight and the storm. Love is in the beginning of things and in the end of them too. Love is the constant that whispers through every season: you are alive, and that is enough.

I used to believe my story would only feel complete if it contained the traditional love story, a partner to walk beside me, a happily ever after to tie it all together. I see now that my story has always been a love story. A love story with God, who never abandoned me. A love story with myself, as I learned to value and forgive the woman I am. A love story with the life I have been entrusted with, in all its highs and lows, its storms and sunrises. This love story is no less real, no less profound, and no less worth celebrating. Love is what I was created from and created for. When I remember that, I realize I am not waiting on some future version of love to arrive. I am already living in the middle of it.

Chapter 17

The Wholeness of a Life Redeemed

When I look back now, it feels almost impossible to reconcile the person I once was with the woman I am today. The memories of pain, chaos, and longing are still there, etched into me like scars that never fade, but they no longer carry the same weight. They are not chains or prisons anymore, but are simply reminders, evidence of the places I have walked through and survived. Evidence that I was broken, but not destroyed. That my life, with all its shattered pieces, has been redeemed in ways I never thought possible.

There was a time when I believed my story would always be defined by struggle and my life would always be measured by what was missing, what was broken, what was too heavy to carry. I thought survival was the best I could hope for, to simply breathe through the pain, patch together the fragments, and make it to the next day. For a long season, that was true. However, redemption has a way of rewriting stories. It doesn't erase the suffering. It transforms it. It doesn't deny the darkness. It shows how light can still break through.

For so many years, I searched for wholeness in all the wrong places. I thought I would find it in validation, achievements, and relationships that promised more than they could ever deliver. I chased it in business, performance, and desperate hope that if I just did enough or became enough, the emptiness inside of me would finally disappear. Every attempt left me emptier, and grasping for more only carved the hollow deeper.

It took losing so much to finally learn what wholeness really meant. It took heartbreak, betrayal, and collapse. It took walking through valleys so dark that I wondered if I would ever find my way out. Slowly, gently, God began to show me that wholeness is not something we earn, and it is not something we can chase down. Wholeness is something we receive. It is the slow mending of what we thought was beyond repair. It is the miracle of realizing that what the world calls ruined, God calls redeemed.

Here is where the truth stuns me still: redemption doesn't just give you back what you lost. It gives you something you never imagined you could hold. I thought the best I could hope for was repair. Instead, I was given renewal. I thought survival was the highest goal. Instead, I was given abundance, not the kind of abundance the world talks about, measured in possessions or achievements, but the kind of abundance that floods your soul with peace when you're sitting in silence, that wraps around you like warmth when you thought you'd always be cold.

There came a moment, not loud or dramatic, when I realized my life had shifted. I was sitting outside as the sun fell low, painting the sky in shades of fire and lavender. I wasn't rushing. I wasn't striving. I was simply still. For the first time in my life, stillness didn't feel like punishment. It felt like a gift. Tears filled my eyes as I whispered to myself, I am not running anymore. That was the moment I knew redemption had not just touched me, it had taken root in me.

The wholeness of a life redeemed is not about the absence of scars. It is about learning to see them as proof of survival. My scars are my story etched in flesh and memory, and I no longer hide them. They tell of nights I thought I would not make it through, and mornings that still somehow came. They tell of losses that threatened to unmake me, and mercies that rebuilt me. They tell of a God who did not leave me where He found me. In the telling, my scars have become sacred.

There is grief, too, and I will not deny it. Redemption does not erase the ache of what was lost. There are versions of myself I will never be again, dreams that died before they bloomed, people I loved who are no longer here to see who I've become. Sometimes, I still feel that ache deep in my chest, like a phantom limb. Even grief has been transformed, no longer swallowing me, but softening me. It keeps me tender, reminding me that life is precious, love is fragile, and nothing is guaranteed. Grief and gratitude now live side by side in me, and together they deepen the soil of my soul.

Maybe that is the mystery of redemption. It doesn't ask us to deny the pain. It asks us to carry it differently, to see it not as the end of the story, but as a passage, blessing even the things that broke us, because without them, we would not have been remade.

What astonishes me most is how redemption alters vision. I look at my life now and see not just what I have gained, but what has been restored within me. The restless hunger has quieted. The striving has ceased. The fear that once dictated my choices has loosened its grip. I no longer live at war with myself. That doesn't mean every day is easy, but it does mean that even in the hard days, I no longer believe the lie that I am alone.

When I think of the woman I was, and the woman I am now, it feels like a resurrection. I was buried under shame, under despair, under fear. And yet, somehow, I rose, not by my own strength, but by grace that refused to let me stay in the grave. That resurrection is the testimony I leave behind: even the most broken life can be redeemed, and even the most shattered soul can be made whole.

I wonder sometimes what my life looks like from the outside. To others, it may appear quiet, even ordinary, but I know the magnitude of the miracle it holds. I know what it means to wake up without panic pressing down on my chest, to breathe without fear constricting my lungs, to live without constantly performing for worth I already possess. To anyone else, this may look simple. To me, it looks like freedom.

Freedom, I have learned, is not loud. It doesn't need to be proven. It is the steady rhythm of a heart finally at rest. It is the courage to love without fear of loss. It is the peace of knowing you are held, even when life is uncertain. It is the quiet triumph of a soul that no longer bows to shame.

Even as I write these words, I feel the depth of something larger than myself. Because this story is mine, yes, but it is also more than mine. It belongs to every person who has ever thought they were too far gone, too scarred, too shattered to be pieced together again. It belongs to the daughters who believe their past disqualifies them, the sons who believe they are trapped in endless cycles, the weary souls who think freedom is for others but never for them. To you, I say: I thought the same. Here I am, breathing proof that there is no life too broken for redemption.

As I reach the end of these pages, I do not see an ending at all. I see a continuation. I see the breath of God still moving, still mending, still calling me deeper into the life He's been writing all along. Though I do not know what storms lie ahead, I know this: my roots are deep now, my faith is steady, my heart is redeemed, and that is enough.

That truth is what I want to leave with you most of all: redemption is not a distant hope, but a present reality. The wholeness I hold today is possible for you too, and that no matter how broken your beginning, your ending can be beautiful.

Because in the end, the story of my life is not about what I lost, but about what was given back to me. Made whole. Made holy. Made new.

This is my testimony.

This is my song.

This is the wholeness of a life redeemed.

Appendix A

Recommended Reading for the Healing Journey

Healing does not happen in isolation, and no single book can hold all the wisdom needed for restoration after trauma, abuse, and loss. Throughout my own journey, I leaned on voices that helped me understand the impact of trauma, reclaim my sense of self, and reconnect with truth, faith, and embodied healing. The books listed here are not quick fixes or surface level encouragement. They are resources that challenged me, supported me, and offered language for experiences I could not yet articulate. If you find yourself resonating with parts of my story, these works may serve as companions as you continue your own path toward wholeness.

The Body Keeps the Score by Bessel Van Der Kolk

This book helped me understand how trauma lives not only in memory, but in the body, and why healing must involve more than willpower or positive thinking.

Waking the Tiger by Peter A. Levine

Levine's work gave me a framework for understanding how trauma becomes trapped in the nervous system and how the body can gently release what the mind cannot force away.

Trauma and Recovery by Judith Herman

This book offered clarity and validation around the stages of trauma recovery and helped me name experiences that once felt chaotic and isolating.

The Soul of Shame by Curt Thompson

Thompson bridges neuroscience and Christian faith, helping me understand how shame forms and how grace and connection are essential to healing.

Healing the Fragmented Selves of Trauma Survivors by Janina Fisher

This book helped me make sense of the inner conflict and fragmentation trauma creates, offering compassion instead of judgment toward parts of myself I once tried to silence.

Boundaries by Henry Cloud and John Townsend

This was instrumental in teaching me that boundaries are not walls or punishments, but necessary expressions of love, responsibility, and self-respect.

Emotionally Healthy Spirituality by Peter Scazzero

This book challenged my tendency to spiritualize pain instead of healing it, showing me that emotional health and spiritual maturity cannot be separated.

The Ragamuffin Gospel by Brennan Manning

This book reminded me of the radical grace of God, especially when shame tried to convince me I was beyond redemption or unworthy of love.

Reflection Questions for Healing and Reclamation

1. When did I first learn to equate safety with control, approval, or submission?
2. What behaviors or patterns have I justified in the name of love that actually diminished me?
3. In what ways have I numbed pain instead of facing it directly?
4. What am I most afraid I would feel if I stopped distracting myself?
5. Where in my life am I performing instead of being present?
6. What parts of myself have I abandoned to survive?
7. How has trauma shaped my understanding of intimacy, safety, and worth?

8. What does my body try to tell me that I have learned to ignore?
9. When have I confused endurance with strength?
10. What boundaries feel hardest for me to set, and why?
11. Where do I still seek validation outside of myself?
12. What would it look like to trust my instincts again?
13. How do I respond when silence forces me to sit with myself?
14. What beliefs about love am I ready to unlearn?
15. In what ways have I minimized my own pain to protect others?
16. What does self-respect look like in my daily decisions?
17. Who am I when no one is watching, approving, or expecting anything from me?
18. What truths have I avoided because they required change?
19. How do I define safety now, apart from another person?
20. What does reclaiming myself mean in this season of my life?

About Kharis Publishing:

Kharis Publishing, an imprint of Kharis Media LLC, is a leading Christian and inspirational book publisher based in Aurora, Chicago metropolitan area, Illinois. Kharis' dual mission is to give voice to under-represented writers (including women and first-time authors) and equip orphans in developing countries with literacy tools. That is why, for each book sold, the publisher channels some of the proceeds into providing books and computers for orphanages in developing countries so that these kids may learn to read, dream, and grow. For a limited time, Kharis Publishing is accepting unsolicited queries for nonfiction (Christian, self-help, memoirs, business, health and wellness) from qualified leaders, professionals, pastors, and ministers.

Learn more at: https://kharispublishing.com/

www.ingramcontent.com/pod-product-compliance
Lightning Source LLC
LaVergne TN
LVHW010619100826
845148LV00014B/3028